Margaret Thatcher

A Margaret Thatcher Biography

Michael Woodford

Table of Contents

"The Iron Lady"

One of the most famous figures in world history was a grocer's daughter who clawed her way to the top of her country's political hierarchy.

At a time when women had defined roles in society and had to grapple with barriers and glass ceilings because of their sex, ambitious and fiery Margaret Hilda Roberts – later, Prime Minister Margaret Thatcher - somehow became (for all of its good and bad) the groundbreaking, trailblazing "Iron Lady."

She did not consider her background or her sex to be a weakness. In fact, she transformed them into a unique proposition. She transformed them into strengths on her way to becoming Europe's first female Prime

Minister. They became part of her brand and iconography, and she sold the sometimes bitter pill of her tough politics with her characteristics.

Britain in the 1970s

Britain in the late-1970s was grappling with many political, economic and cultural changes. Decades of affluence post-war had given way to a nation struggling to compete on the world stage. It was not one of the country's finer moments, and there was a sense of it being a declining empire.

Memories of those years past are notoriously bleak, and Margaret Thatcher – whether justly or unjustly – is often credited for national salvation. David Cameron, Prime Minister from 2010 to 2016, honored Margaret Thatcher with a bold tribute stating she *"didn't just lead…she saved our country."* It is a sentiment held by many.

Before she came into the office, inflation was in double-digits and taking a huge chunk out of the value of people's earnings. When she became Prime Minister in 1979, inflation was at 10.3 percent per year.

There were crippling strikes aplenty from trade unions. 1.4 million people – 5.3 percent of the workforce – did not have jobs in 1979. State-owned industries were not at their most efficient. When she came to power, the state had ownership and control in the industries of coal, electricity, gas, petroleum, steel, telecom and water. Government debt was high too, at 43.6 percent of GDP in 1979.

Margaret Thatcher set to work controlling runaway inflation. She withstood striking unions and in one famous case, called their bluff and did not blink for a year until they gave up. Her government worked on union reform. Her policies helped shift her country from the manufacturing industry to services.

Her free market vision privatized many industries.

Many of the changes she made were so profound that they were regarded as irreversible, inherited by the governments that succeeded hers, and the effects of which are still apparent up to now.

Loved and Hated

The results of her 11 years in office actualizing her stern, self-reliant, some say individualistic worldview leave her with a mixed legacy.

For her critics, trade union reform left unions practically impotent and the working class with less bargaining power over corporations. Deregulation led to reckless and risky financial behavior that has repeatedly endangered whole economies. Many communities dependent on manufacturing lost their main source of livelihood and never fully recovered. Some critics even blame her and the loyal proponents of her Thatcherism for crafting a country divided both in rhetoric as well as in economic class.

Many people felt left behind, even when the economy was recovering and corporations were excelling. Some felt the working classes were bearing the bitter pill of her sweeping reforms while the rich were less burdened.

Her complex politics eventually led to protests on the streets, divisions within her own party and eventually, her resignation.

Love her or hate her, what cannot be denied is that Margaret Thatcher inherited a tough situation and she had to be tough right back in pretty much every imaginable respect – in the climb to her position, the maintenance of her position, and in doing the actual work of attempting to improve her country's condition. She was patriotic and hard-working, often having 18-hour days. She also paid the price in sacrificing irrecoverable time and close relationships with her family.

Indeed, given all the costs, the Prime Minister's job can be considered a bitter prize for the precious few who could win it.

British politics was still an old boys' club when Margaret Hilda Roberts came into the picture. She had her taste of rejections and defeats, and the wins when they finally came did not come easy. All the while she had to face double standards, suffering personal attacks aside from fending off those lobbied against her politics.

She was considered frosty, abrasive and combative, where a male politician would have likely just gotten away with firmly asserting his will. Comments were made on her hair, on her clothes, on her voice. As one Conservative commenter was quoted by

Time in 1975, she was "*the wrong sort of woman.*"

Her work also took a toll on her personal life. When she came into power in 1979, she was married and a mother of twins. Her demanding work would present challenges and lost opportunities for bonding with her family, especially with her children.

As for her beloved husband, being married to one of the most powerful women in the world could not have been easy, on top of his own concerns as a millionaire businessman. At some point, their union was even be plagued by rumors of the possibility of a divorce.

Indeed, it was not easy being an "Iron Lady" at the pinnacle of British politics on the world stage. Margaret Thatcher had to leap fences and defy the odds at almost every step of the way.

As we all know, her unlikely ascension to power was only the beginning. She also had to push a bold, broad vision for her country that was not uncontroversial (to say the least!), and would lead her people to irreversible changes.

Her politics and economics of small government, privatization, deregulation and self-reliance courted and still courts strenuous opposition, and she had to make hard calls in hard times.

But even her critics would have to admit that she had courage and cunning, and she helped usher in some much-needed modernity to struggling segments of the economy.

Her name would eventually be given to a modern and powerful political philosophy that still carries a certain appeal in our present time: Thatcherism.

All but a few politicians in all the countries of the world can boast of having a trademark vision, captured in a single word.

She, in short, made history.

This is hers.

The Early Years

Everyone had to start from somewhere. But for a woman who spent 11 years at the much-coveted address of 10 Downing Street sitting on the hard-won Prime Minister seat, the unlikely beginnings could be found in a politically-active grocer's home in the market town of Grantham.

Childhood and Faith

Margaret Hilda Roberts was born on the 13th of October, 1925 in Grantham, Lincolnshire, England. She was the daughter of shopkeeper, Methodist lay preacher and alderman (later, mayor) Alfred Roberts and his wife, Beatrice. The family lived above the shop, where Margaret was sometimes spotted behind the counter.

Alfred Roberts was a powerful influence in Margaret's life. She credited him for *"all the things that I do believe."* At 6 feet and 3 inches tall with a voice made for sermons, he cut a striking speaker, and had actually toured Methodist circles for sermons. Margaret was often with him.

Her home life and the father who headed it, shaped much of the "iron" character the world would eventually come to know. The Methodist faith followed by the family and preached by her father has even been regarded by some political and religious pundits as the roots of "Thatcherism."

While this may sound surprising, it should be noted that one of the most famous quotes attributed to Margaret Thatcher is, *"Economics is the method; the object is to change the soul."* She also described in an interview that the underlying foundation of a democracy is not only the vote of a majority but beyond that, into morality – *"the belief that the majority of people are good and decent."* In short, there was a spiritual component to the way she looked at the world and how she governed her country.

But before she had her chance to meddle with the "method" as a Prime Minister, she lived with her family in a close-knit community and they were active in a congregation espousing shared values of free will, self-help and social involvement.

A typical Sunday for the Roberts sisters (Margaret and older sister Muriel), for example, comprised of both religious instruction and services, with restrictions on games and entertainment (even sewing!).

Beyond Sundays – for the future PM would say in an interview that her faith was not *"only a faith for Sundays,"* they also had social events around the congregation like the Youth Guild, and were raised on daily cleanliness, discipline, and duty. They prayed before and after eating, and were teetotalers. The woman who eventually became Prime Minister though, would later frequently enjoy whisky, which she found energizing and fortifying.

Either way, their faith was therefore a very deep, important and regular part of their lives.

Margaret's father Alfred Roberts, an in-demand lay preacher, had actually delivered sermons against avarice and extolled the values of thrift, self-reliance and a good work ethic. He also had distinct views on the freedom of the individual – which likely had a bearing on Margaret Thatcher's eventual belief in a free market. Methodism, after all, was a religion that the future PM would describe as a practical as well as an evangelical faith.

Her family's religious background and its belief in the individual – that the person's faith and accountability is ultimately between him and his God, that the Ten Commandments were addressed to individuals rather than collectives, that choices and actions should be left to the individual rather than to a larger body like the state - was not at odds with capitalism if pursued with altruism. She once noted there was nothing wrong in wealth creation; instead, what was wrong was in *the love of money…"*

Having funds after all, was what allowed a person to share in the first place. The founder of Methodism, John Welsey, was known for promoting hard work, thriftiness and saving, so that one may have the resources with which to be generous to the needy.

Margaret Thatcher's individualistic approach is also probably why in her later career, she was personally conservative but generally hands-off in matters that can be considered as areas of personal morality and conscience. Among these are divorce, abortion and sexuality.

Her faith also likely shaped her stance in the era's cause *du jour* – the Cold War. Communism after all, had been more about the state rather than the individual, and was not moved by faith in a god. She stood against communism abroad and against socialism on the domestic front, in what many look upon as a believable extension of her religious belief in individual liberty.

Margaret Thatcher's politics did not always align with Methodism along the course of her more than 11-year tenure as Prime Minister of course, and she later drifted closer to the formality of Anglicanism. Though some do say the shift may have been political, what with Tories being more linked with the Anglicans.

At any rate, as can be noted above, strokes of her father and their Methodist beliefs could be seen in the formation of the character and world view of the future Prime Minister.

Her perspectives were also likely formed by the harsh circumstances in which she and her community lived.

Her country was still coming from the ravages of the Great War of 1914-1918, and leading up to the Second World War which eventually broke out in 1939. There was peace by the time she turned 20 years old in 1945, but many men had been killed and there was also unemployment. But she, her family, their community and their country, just had to work hard and find a way to move forward.

Her childhood in Grantham imbued in her a sense of community, good neighborliness and civic duty and pride, which she would carry with her into her political career.

Education and Work Experience

Margaret Thatcher studied in state schools several miles away from home, which she walked to even as a young girl. She was a good student and got into Oxford University when she was 18 years old.

She had a fine, scientific mind. Her educational background was in Chemistry, which she studied at Somerville College in Oxford. One of her professors was the Nobel Prize winner, Dorothy Hodgkin.

Studying wasn't all she did at university, however. She became active in the Wesley Memorial chapel and lent her voice to preaching, but later became more active in politics. She cut her teeth at the Oxford University Conservative Association, which she eventually spearheaded as president (not the first female to do so, however; she was the third). Her involvement in the association allowed her to make Conservative connections that served her political career later.

She continued to be active in politics after graduation. Even when she moved to Colchester and was employed by a plastics company, she was still linked with the local organization of the Conservative Party. She also worked in the field of chemistry in Dartford.

Interestingly, Margaret Thatcher may be best known for her politics, but she also has another achievement. She, as part of a team at a chemistry company, helped develop ice cream additives and emulsifiers that made soft serve possible. Margaret Thatcher ultimately earned a reputation for being frigid, but it might surprise people to know she was involved in literal ice cream too!

First Political Forays

Her initial forays into elected office were unsuccessful. She became a prospective Conservative candidate for Dartford in Kent in 1949, but lost in the general elections of 1950 and 1951. It was at any rate, considered a "safe" Labour seat, a fact the savvy young pol was aware of but nevertheless fought through.

A community's party leanings wasn't her only challenge. She was young and a woman, where politics was male-dominated. But while the runs were unsuccessful, they increased her public profile. She wasn't just a promising young female; she was at the time, the *youngest* Conservative candidate ever. Margaret Roberts was a good story the media couldn't help but follow.

It wasn't just media attention that she gleaned from the unsuccessful initial forays into elected office. These also provided the encounters by which she would catch the eye of businessman, Denis Thatcher.

Love and Family

Denis Thatcher was born on the 10th of May, 1910 in Lewisham, London, England. The family's roots however, go back to the coastal town of Wanganui in New Zealand.

There, his grandfather made a fortune on weed killers for the railways. His father then put up a similar business endeavor in the U.K. for general chemicals and married a fellow entrepreneur, Lillian Bird.

Denis was sent to boarding school from age 8, first at Bognor Regis and then to Mill Hill. He wasn't the most remarkable of scholars, but excelled in sports like cricket and rugby.

He eventually finished school and headed off for work in the family business.

Even with his family at the helm, he was expected to work his way to the top. One of his duties brought him to Germany in 1937, where he got the sense that World War II was brewing.

When hostilities began exactly as he had expected them to, he was an army officer. He was, however, on the staff side due to poor eyesight. But by 1945 he was a Major at the British HQ in Marseilles, and had distinguished himself enough to be made a Member of the Order of the British Empire.

He also managed to get married and divorced…

His wife, the trailblazing Margaret Thatcher wasn't always the first in everything. The first Mrs. Denis Thatcher was Ms. Margaret Kempson, a beauty Denis wed in March

1942. They, however, never had the chance to live together because of the war and were divorced by 1948.

Denis thrived in the army, but left post-war to head his family's business. When his father fell ill in 1949, he became the managing director.

He met the spirited Margaret Roberts, then an Oxford research chemist, along the course of a dinner dance in 1950.

He was attracted to her and aside from his character, was a successful businessman and a millionaire as well – he had his own appeal. He was however divorced, with a known taste for gin. Not quite the Methodist poster boy, but his business acumen and some say resemblance to Margaret's father, eventually won her over too. He proposed in 1951 and she said yes. They married at Wesley's Chapel in London that year.

It may be recalled that this was also the year of her failed second try at entering parliament. But in gaining Denis Thatcher as a partner for life, she was blessed. He had the self-possession and confidence in his own assets and achievements to be comfortable being married to a powerful and ambitious woman. He also had the financial means to allow her to focus on her political career and take it to the next level.

After marriage, they honeymooned in Madeira, Paris and Portugal. She then studied law in 1952 and prepared for the Bar, becoming a barrister in 1953. It was quite the feat, especially since their twins, Mark and Carol were also born in that year. She famously sent in her application for the Bar finals while still in the hospital!

Aside from being a barrister, a wife, a mother to twins and a politically active citizen, Margaret Thatcher was also known for cooking.

Even when she was the Prime Minister, she reportedly did not hire a chef and somehow managed to make time to prepare meals for her husband. Sometimes, even her cabinet members got a taste of her culinary efforts.

Political Rise

For Margaret Thatcher, being a homemaker was not unlike housekeeping a country. Understanding "*the problems of running a home*" can bring one closer to "*understanding the problems of running a country.*"

She was comfortable in being both a female, a mother and a leader at the same time. She brought in a type of pragmatic, tough, home-style sensibility to the otherwise lofty position of a politician… and the lofty intentions she had for her country.

Her first television interview, for example, had been with her then-six-year-old twins sitting on the arms of her chair.

From the Shadows

Margaret Thatcher's losses in 1950 and 1951 did not deter her from continuing her pursuit of a political career. She tried to become the Conservative candidate for Orpington (also in Kent) in 1954, but was rejected. It wouldn't be until years later that she finally found her place in the sun.

She could have quit after Orpington, but in 1956, she expressed her desire to be a candidate again. Party selection committees had a hard time conceiving of political victory from a young woman with two kids, but in 1958, she applied for the "safe" Conservative seat of Finchley and was selected.

It was not without controversy and the result was met with dissatisfaction from some corners. But by 1959, Mrs. Thatcher, mother of twins, finally made her way into the Commons as MP for Finchley.

In 1960, she became Parliamentary Secretary at the Ministry of Pensions and National Insurance in Harold Macmillan's government.

The Conservatives lost in the government when Harold Wilson become Prime Minister in the mid-1960s. Margaret Thatcher, however, continued to hold prominent roles within her party, using her fine mind and education in posts working on taxes, fuel and power, and transport.

In 1969, she became the Shadow Education Secretary. With Edward Heath's surprising election victory for the Conservatives in 1970, she became the Secretary of State for Education and Science.

She was regarded as a good worker, an effective administrator. But by late-1971, she had acquired the unfortunate title of "Margaret Thatcher Milk Snatcher." It was not an unjust title because while she was in this role, children did lose access to free school milk. For a time, Margaret Thatcher may have even been, in the words of the newspaper *The Sun*, "*The Most Unpopular Woman in Britain.*"

Her rationale for the move was to make a really relatively paltry savings of £9 million in public expenditure, so that she could protect the more educational elements of her budget. Good intentions aside, the unfortunate title still stuck. It was a learning experience for the politician and she was reportedly miserable for a time.

This was likely exacerbated by her relations with the beleaguered Prime Minister Heath, who held the position from 1970 to 1974. They famously did not get along in the best of terms, partly because she reportedly had trouble engaging him with her ideas. It may also be because of the difference in their political views even if they were from the same party.

Edward Heath was himself a barrier-breaker. He was the Oxford-educated, World War II vet and son of a carpenter, who rose to Conservative Party leadership as among the first in modernity not to have come from the upper-classes. His 1970 win in the general elections was a surprise over Labour, but his time at the head of the country's political leadership was marked by a lot of economic difficulties and political challenge from his own party.

He faced strikes from powerful trade unions, rising oil prices (there was conflict in the Middle East at the time) and inflation. He had to make tough choices too, among them a political "U-turn" that deviated from some of his party's beliefs.

Senior Conservatives on the right-wing side, Margaret Thatcher among them, felt he should not have compromised and/or his compromises were not effective.

Margaret Thatcher's steely resolve and refusal to bend (both a strength and weakness) would always be a part of her character. In one of her most memorable speeches, she was quoted as saying, "*You turn if you want to. The lady's not for turning.*"

Heath fell even further from power with the hits taken by the Conservatives in the February and then the October 1974 elections. Someone from the party seemed bound to challenge him, it was just a matter of who would do it and when.

Keith Joseph was one of these men, who shared some of Margaret Thatcher's views and with whom she had a good friendship. In the meantime, Margaret Thatcher received another high-profile post, shadowing the Department of the Environment.

Joseph set up the Centre for Policy Studies ("CPS"), which revolved around free market thinking. He also involved his friend, Margaret Thatcher. Around this time, she seemed to believe that Joseph would be the Conservative party's candidate.

It was an understandable assumption, and one made by many. That was, until a tactless remark by Joseph regarding babies born to adolescent moms from the lower social classes made the rounds and severely impacted his chances.

Elsewhere, Margaret Thatcher was improving her own. In a shadow cabinet reshuffle under the beleaguered Heath, she found another role with which to shine. She gave a stellar performance in speaking for the Opposition during Budget debates.

But mounting a challenge against Heath would still be an uphill climb for her, if not a seemingly impossible feat. He reportedly responded to Thatcher telling him of her intent to challenge him by turning away, shrugging and saying, "*If you must.*"

Margaret Thatcher's rise to the top of party leadership was thereafter aided by a number of factors. Edward duCann, who could have been another (and perhaps more significant) challenger, did not do so. The person who likely would have managed duCann's campaign, Airey Neave, reportedly had issues with Heath and so offered his expertise to Thatcher. He was the kind of savvy, strategic and well-networked political player she needed on her side. At the end of the day, perhaps some of their members just wanted Heath out instead of actually wanting Thatcher in.

The result was the same. Whatever their motivation, the party allowed Thatcher to best Heath and in another round of votes, other runners-up. She became Leader of the Opposition in 1975.

The Leader of Opposition

By 1975, Margaret Thatcher secured the Conservative party leadership. She was the first female opposition leader in the House of Commons, and she would be in this position for four years.

Broadly speaking, the Conservatives in the Opposition and the Labour in Government held different beliefs on the right approach to their country's myriad of economic problems. For the Conservatives, there had to be less government control, less taxation, less spending and trade union reform.

The Labour party had a number of years with which to give their solutions a shot, while the opposing Conservatives fought for their own philosophy.

Margaret Thatcher didn't do too badly going up against the leadership of Harold Wilson and then James Callaghan after him, but she could often come across as shrill in her performances.

Aside from going against opposing views on the other side of the aisle, she also had to deal with difficulties in managing her own party. She built a relatively moderate shadow cabinet, and had even offered a post to Heath (he declined to her relief). She had also engaged some of the men she bested in the leadership race, William Whitelaw and Geoffrey Howe.

Politics was a battle with many fronts. One had to rise above the other stars in one's own party, outperform the opposing one, and all this politicking comes on top of the actual governance of a country still plagued by economic woes.

In the leadership now with like-minded men like Joseph and Howe, Thatcher tried to envision and enact a solution. Of particular concern around this time were the trade unions, which embroiled the country in the so-called "Winter of Discontent" strikes held in 1978 to 1979.

Along the course of her work at this point of her thriving career, Margaret Thatcher's performances had caught the attention of not only Conservatives and the general public, but also that of a powerful foreign eye. *Red Star*, the Soviet Army magazine, referred to her disparagingly as "The Iron Lady" following a defense speech made in 1976.

Now this was a title she actually liked. The image would always trail her from that point onward. It would even be the title of the acclaimed 2011 biopic about her life, which starred (and secured another Academy Award for) Meryl Streep.

But long before she lived a life crafted for the movies, the Margaret Thatcher of the mid-to-late-1970s worked on securing the position that would make her a legend.

Back at the home front… at around the same time that she was crawling up toward her peak in politics, her more than decade-older husband, Denis, was retiring. His business activities had actually been decreasing for years, while her political responsibilities gradually picked up.

He had sold his company and got decent returns for himself as well as a part in the purchasing parent company's board. But by the mid-1970s, work like this was easing up too.

It was perhaps a good thing. As the husband of the leader of the opposition and later the

Prime Minister, Denis Thatcher was expected to be by her side in many occasions. This was especially true when her job took her to foreign shores or required her to entertain.

Perhaps more importantly, she he functioned as an invaluable sounding board and wellspring of wise counsel for her behind closed doors. Publicly however, he was discreet, stalwart in his loyalty, and made a steadfast companion for so powerful and willful a woman.

"The Iron Lady" at Work

In the late-1970s, the public was weary and impatient following "The Winter of Discontent."

The Labour Party was beginning to look impotent against the union problems and amidst other economic challenges. Perhaps the Conservative campaign, the rather clever

"Labour Isn't Working" line, really resonated too, for the nation was going to try a different approach to their years' long problems.

Labour's lackluster performance helped propel the Conservatives back in power by 1979. Party leader, Margaret Thatcher, landed the role (and record first female!) of being Prime Minister.

From her spot at the top, she finally had the muscle to push harder for her right-wing, pro-business, trade union reform beliefs.

And so the years 1979 to 1989 featured a wide-scale shift away from state-control toward a freer business model. Controls in enterprise, pricing, dividends, wages and exchange were either limited or abandoned. The early results of these and their other efforts at economic policy, especially in taming inflation, were mixed.

An oil price hike, which contributed to an international recession, helped matters not at all. But the government under Thatcher stuck by its restrictive monetary policies. They raised income tax too. Unemployment rose – brutally, and urban riots broke out.

The economy at home already would have been a challenge for anyone (just ask Edward Heath), without difficulties mounted both from within and from without.

Thatcher had to face attacks from the Conservative party, sometimes from her own Cabinet. One of her economic strategies was soundly denounced in *The Times* by hundreds of economists.

From abroad, Thatcher's first term was also plagued by Argentina attacking the Falkland Islands. It was a British territory off the coast of Argentina that had been a point of contention between the two countries. The Falklands War, which would begin with

Argentinian invasion in April 1982, turned the Prime Minister toward international affairs when she had previously been very focused on the domestic front.

"The Iron Lady," however, shone as a war leader. She acted quickly and decisively, and supported her military materially and politically. The Falklands War ended with the Argentinian surrender of June the same year it began – bringing victory and prestige for the Prime Minister and Britain. It also likely brought the Conservatives another victory during the elections of 1983… that, along with some measure of economic recovery.

Margaret Thatcher also had to deal with aggression closer to home. In 1984, an assassination attempt by the Irish Republican Army saw a bomb planted at the site of the Conservative Conference, a hotel in Brighton.

"The Iron Lady" showed her mettle with a speech the next day and the conference continued… even when some of those hurt in the blast had been her friends.

Her second term, from 1983 to 1987, also showed her keeping up with the international community's hardest-hitters at such an important time for global change.

She was a staunch ally of United States President Ronald Reagan, with whom she shared conservative and anti-communist beliefs. Together, they showed a strong Western alliance. She held meetings and formed a friendship with the Soviet Leader, Mikhail Gorbachev and hailed him as someone with whom one 'can do business.' She was also in talks with the China's Deng Xiao Ping, making important arrangements regarding the fate of British-administered Hong Kong and establishing the Anglo-Chinese Joint Agreement.

Political Decline

The road there was painful and bumpy, but the economy was recovering and growing. Thatcher's government had withstood a year-long miners' strike. The country looked like a promising investment again.

Furthermore, the Leader of the Opposition, Neil Kinnock, wasn't quite up to par and ultimately proved unconvincing. The Prime Minister had also become a world player, with close connections to the leaders of the United States of America and the Soviet Union.

Thus, the June 1987 election was still a victory for the Conservatives and Margaret Thatcher. She landed her third term in the office of the Prime Minister, but it would be her last.

"No, no, no..."

There were many reasons why Margaret Thatcher's time as Prime Minister and Conservative party leader were coming to a close.

One of them was that she harbored anti-Euro rhetoric that was not aligned with the views of not just many in her party but even within her own team. Her stance was typified by her infamous *"No, no, no"* response before the House of Commons and European Commission Chief Jacques Delors in 1990.

One of the key figures in her downfall is widely regarded to be Geoffrey Howe. It may be recalled from earlier that she and Howe shared some views on the economy and indeed, he was not just a part of her government but a very influential one. He had even been described as a close confidant to "The Iron Lady."

Howe was at different points of Thatcher's leadership, chancellor, foreign secretary, leader of the House and deputy prime minister. He was also co-architect of many of the economic policies that helped put Margaret Thatcher's name in the history books.

Their relationship soured over their divergent views on Britain's participation in a more centralized Europe. One of the techniques Howe reportedly employed to convince the Prime Minister to do what he believed was the right course of action was to threaten her with resignation. He is said to have done this at one time, alongside Chancellor Nigel Lawson.

Ganging up on "The Iron Lady" (even if she sometimes gave way) did not come without a price. Their relationship and trust deteriorated and she shifted Howe's role in what was widely seen as a demotion.

The relationship seemed bound to sour at any rate, with Howe worried about Thatcher's somewhat confrontational attitude on Europe.

Her stance can probably be best encased by her "Bruges Speech" of 1988. She believed in a future with Europe, and her free enterprise slant was congruent with international economic liberty in a competitive market. But she also harbored concerns over how European supranationalism could come at the cost of sovereignty, especially with the seemingly socialist-leaning direction of the European leadership at the time. In her view, they have just *"rolled back the frontiers of the state in Britain,"* as the speech went. Why would they wish to be similarly imposed upon *"at European level, with a new European super-state exercising a new dominance…"*

It was in short, "*no, no, no.*"

Thatcher and Howe had very different opinions. But where she could be abrasive, Howe was generally regarded as mild, quiet and sometimes even bumbling. He was not an electrifying speaker and did not translate well on television. One politico compared confrontation with Howe as "*being savaged by a dead sheep.*"

But this perhaps made the resignation speech he delivered all the more striking and memorable. It was a brutal, incisive piece that is often thought of as the precursor to Thatcher's own resignation shortly afterwards.

He delivered it with calm conviction, but it was blistering in content. It was a savage takedown and perhaps, as *ITV* called it in 2015, "*the speech which ultimately destroyed Margaret Thatcher.*"

Howe lamented her perception of Europe as a *"nightmare"* and how that view could present *"increasingly serious risks for the future of our nation."* He also compared her to a team leader sabotaging the efforts of her own members – *"…sending your opening batsmen to the crease only for them to find… their bats have been broken before the game by the team captain."*

Those loyal to Thatcher thought of the speech as treachery, a betrayal. Others found Howe courageous in fighting for what he honestly believed was right, and in being the first to really stand up against "The Iron Lady" when she was wrong.

Reactions to Howe's speech will probably heavily depend on how one thinks of Margaret Thatcher… If she was right she must have been betrayed; if she was not, a man of integrity had finally found the courage to stand up for what he believed in.

Even years later, this is still being debated.

The Community Charge Tax

What is indisputable is that Howe's fiery (though coldly delivered) speech helped set off Thatcher's decline, and she was challenged for the leadership by Michael Heseltine shortly afterwards. Discontent was at any rate brewing even before then, and Thatcher's anti-Euro rhetoric was just one part of the picture.

She seemed out-of-touch and decreasing in relevance. On the international scene, the Soviet Union collapsed and Cold War warriors like her became regarded somewhat as relics. She had been close with United States President Ronald Reagan, but when George Bush came into office after the Gipper, they did not share the same camaraderie and shared differing views on

German reunification and its place in the European power structure.

But perhaps most damaging was that back home, she wasn't very popular either. In the Community Charge or Poll Tax, Margaret Thatcher had perhaps finally championed one radical and bitter policy too many.

Support for her – and the pols in her party - corroded with a proposed, fixed rate local tax. It was profoundly unpopular in the public and divisive in the government.

Prior to the Community Charge Tax was the "Rates." "The Rates" was basically a tax system that allowed the local council to levy charges on the populace depending on house rental value. The purpose of the Rates was to have funding for community services and infrastructure.

The Thatcher-backed new tax system introduced by the Conservatives basically still collected funds for the same community purposes as the Rates, and amounts were still to be determined by local authorities. The major difference, however, was that the tax would be a flat rate charged to each adult (hence the moniker, "Poll Tax"). It spared students and unemployed from the burden, but was profoundly unpopular for several reasons.

First, it was believed that flat fees benefited the rich and burdened the poor. Second, big families in small homes felt they were shouldering disproportionately heavy charges. Third, because there was a lot of discretion on the local council level, it was open to overcharging.

Public discontent reached a fever pitch in London in 1990, when a protest march devolved into a riot that left 45 policemen hurt and 340 people arrested.

The level of dismay inspired by the new tax system not only created chaos in the streets, it also endangered the electoral prospects of the Conservative party, whose members were associated with the negativity. And yet with regards to the controversial tax, Thatcher seemed unbending and insistent.

This was therefore what Margaret Thatcher – not a particularly warm or loved politician to begin with – was looking at in 1990. An unremarkable international position. Unrest in the streets from an unpopular tax. Divisions in a party that may lose its position of power. Dissent in her own ranks.

She suddenly surprisingly made an easy target.

Michael Heseltine challenged her for party leadership in 1990. She bested him, but with an indecisive margin that still required a second round. The writings were on the wall. Support for her was wavering. It was enough for her to recognize it was time to step down.

Margaret Thatcher as Prime Minister had never lost an election… but she was basically unceremoniously dumped by her own Conservative Party.

She would always be sour on the circumstances of her downfall and looked upon it as treachery, just as many of her supporters do. She was said to be even more angered by was its poor timing. Saddam Hussein had invaded Kuwait, U.S. President Bush was involved in the conflict, and he was beginning to engage with her expertise. She therefore felt compelled to exit the political stage at a time when the country was on the brink armed conflict.

She announced her resignation on the 22nd of November, 1990. She basically cited the following reasons for her departure: party unity, as well as better "*prospects of victory in a General Election*" for the Conservatives, if she stepped down.

She was out of Number 10 Downing Street by November 28th.

Love and Marriage in the Spotlight

Politics can be consuming and as seen above, brutal and sometimes unforgiving. Sometimes, the only safe space a pol can ultimately rely upon is home.

But by its own consuming nature, politics can take a heavy toll on a politician's personal life. In 1995, Margaret Thatcher spoke of how such an occupation could be detrimental to family.

Home life for the Thatchers wasn't all smooth sailing, even before she became Prime Minister.

Sometimes in the 1960s, Margaret's husband Denis had a nervous breakdown. It might have been due to overwork at the family business alongside his drinking; these are at least what he himself had speculated in discussing the incident with a biographer, along with the heavy pressure of keeping his mother, sister and aunt financially secure.

It is not known if his wife's absorbing political work had anything to do with it (he never openly blamed her pursuit of her career), but a high stress job that limited her availability could not have helped matters much.

Their daughter Carol, had spoken with an authorized biographer of her father's dislike *"being married to a politician"* for a time. Splitting up may have even been in the cards, though this is unverified. Denis eventually became more and more comfortable with his role though. A refreshing break and retirement may have had a lot to do with it.

He recovered from his breakdown by taking a two-month vacation overseas, and eventually sold his company to lessen the work pressure while he slid more and more into being a rising star's husband.

This temporary setback aside, for the most part Sir Denis Thatcher played his designated role well. He may have even summed it best when he said a prime minister's consort was *"always present, never there."*

He had considerable wealth, preoccupations and achievements all on his own. As a matter of fact, early in the morning after his wife won Conservative opposition leadership in 1975, he was at his office, as if it were any other day. He continued to be busy with directorships until he retired.

He also appeared to have the personality of a man who could handle standing beside or even in the shadow of a powerful woman.

Over time, he acquired a firmer understanding of his role and what was expected of him. He was loyal to her and publicly discrete (he declined interviews), while providing her with counsel behind closed doors. In her autobiography, Margaret Thatcher lauded these same traits in her husband, describing him as "*a fund of shrewd advice…sensibly saved… for me rather than the outside world.*"

What he did show the world though, was that he could approach his role as Britain's first male consort to the Prime Minister with humor and charm. He was known for a bawdy joke and quick, irreverent quips. His wife's position, for example, he had once described as "*a temporary job.*"

He suffered the occasional verbal faux pas too, but was generally uncontroversial. And while he eschewed interviews, he was friendly to the press.

He managed what is widely regarded as a difficult position with easy grace, even when he was often lampooned and caricatured in the press. The millionaire oil executive, if he minded, did not seem to be too riled and even had jokes about his own alcohol, cigarette and golf habits.

He occupied himself as a support to his wife, and was by her side in many of her trips abroad, including those to South Africa and the battlefields of the Falklands. He was also quietly involved in plenty of charities. He was granted a baronetcy in 1990 for his contributions.

At the time of Denis Thatcher's death at age 88 in June 2003, Prime Minister Tony Blair referred to him as kind and generous, "*a real gentleman.*" Iain Duncan Smith, then leader of the Conservatives, praised him as "*what was best in the wartime generation.*"

But greater and sweeter than any praise from illustrious figures is how *his* "Iron Lady" wife thought of him. The former PM once referred to her husband as the "*golden thread*" wound across her life.

He died at a London hospital, with his famous wife and twin children by his side.

"The Iron Lady" as a Mother

Margaret Thatcher as Prime Minister seemed to have the vibe of a stern taskmaster, not only to the men she commanded but the country she led. One can only imagine what she would have been like as a mother.

We can never really know what goes on behind closed doors, but most can't help but wonder - how could she have been like as a mom to twins Carol and Mark?

It may be interesting to note that Margaret Thatcher herself did not have the warmest relationship with her own mother, Beatrice Roberts.

In the 1990s, Margaret Thatcher released a thick memoir and yet barely mentioned Beatrice, especially compared to how she had celebrated her father, Alfred Roberts. It was not Beatrice's only apparent absence in the politician's consciousness, a phenomenon which became a matter of public (sometimes wild) speculation.

In a 1961 interview, Margaret had professed her love for her mother, even though she also said that, "*…after I was 15 we had nothing more to say to each other.*"

This might have been due to Margaret being a younger sister (to Muriel), with the elder having first command of their mother's attention. It may have also been due to fundamental personality differences that let Margaret identify with her father much better.

Nothing much is known about "Beatie" as Beatrice was called. She was born in Grantham in 1888 to parents Daniel Stephenson (a cloakroom attendant) and Phoebe Crust (who worked in a factory). She was brought up in a strict household and was also a regular attendee at Sunday services.

She had some cooking and baking skills. The skills she shared with Margaret; the food she made she shared with the less fortunate. In latter interviews, Margaret Thatcher seemed to be able to say very little about her, other than that she was a generous, practical woman who kept her opinions to herself.

Quite different indeed from Margaret! So how was her relationship with her own children, given her notoriously demanding work, and the vague relationship she had with her own mom?

When Carol and Mark – twins two minutes apart – were born, their mother Margaret was 27 years old and on the brink of breaking into politics.

It was August 1953, and their mom wouldn't become the Conservative representative for Finchley in North London for a few more years. But she was still busy and not unlike other families of the Thatchers' stature, availed of the care of a full-time nanny.

Parents generally do not admit to favorites and Margaret has been described as a loving mother to both her kids, but it was believed by many that Mark was hers. He brought out a light in her eye and a notable note in her voice.

This reportedly did not escape Carol, who has been quoted as saying, *"Mark was certainly the star"* and writing how she harbored feelings of being *"second of the two."*

Carol seemed to harbor complex feelings about her vaunted mother. She studied law, moved countries and became a successful media personality. She is a journalist and broadcaster, and had also featured in the ITV show, *I'm a Celebrity… Get Me Out of Here!*

But she also believed that her achievements wouldn't be enough for anyone to *"ever know me for being anything other than Margaret Thatcher's daughter…"*

She never felt unloved though. One of the more endearing stories about how Margaret Thatcher could be both PM and mom at the same time was when Carol had a relationship with then-MP John Aitken. The couple made plans to go on holiday, but he was suddenly faced with an important political vote that would have jeopardized their travel arrangements. Carol's mom, Opposition leader at the time, shuffled their political business around discretely for her daughter's sake. Unfortunately, nothing flourished of Carol's and Aitken's relationship.

Carol proved dutiful a daughter too. Even if she felt that Mark was the favorite, she was said to be the one who mostly looked after their mother in Margaret Thatcher's final years.

The siblings had a strained relationship that is said to have escalated into a real feud following their mother's passing.

Carol had arranged for an auction of their mother's things, which reportedly infuriated her brother Mark. Some people questioned Carol's motives, believing the sale to be profit-driven and opportunistic, while Mark worried about the preservation of the

Margaret Thatcher legacy. In contrast to Carol, he was said to have hung onto what their mother had left him.

It was not the first time the siblings had differing views on their mother's legacy and how it was to be preserved. Mark was also reportedly in dismay over some parts of Carol's 2008 memoir, *A Swim-on Part in the Goldfish Bowl*, which contained details on their mother's dementia.

Not that Mark was completely saintly himself. He failed accountancy exams. He acquired a reputation as a playboy. He showed some recklessness; he was missing for days in the 1980s along the course of driving a rally in the Sahara. He eventually became a rich businessman, and while he seems to have achieved the feat cleanly, it was tainted by the impression of several observers who attributed it to his use of connections. Most notably in 2004, he became linked to a controversial coup attempt in international affairs.

In her later years, Margaret Thatcher confided in her official biographer, the journalist Charles Moore, about her more private regrets. Mr. Moore has been quoted as saying his subject worried about having "*failed her children*" or having been "*an unsuccessful mother.*"

This is probably one of the few ways the otherwise singular Margaret Thatcher is like a lot of other working women (no matter the career), especially mothers. There is a so-called 'double burden' of being expected to do well at work, without a reduction in expectations from the home front.

In Margaret Thatcher's case, she (perhaps just as much or even more than society) had a lot of expectations of herself. According to her daughter Carol, "*she never relaxed,*" doing household chores quickly so that she could turn to the correspondences and speechwriting required of her parliamentary position. Carol called her a "*superwoman before the phrase had been invented*."

Aside from helping to run a country, Margaret Thatcher was also involved in a litany of more homely pursuits. Among them – cooking for her husband and personally wallpapering Carol and Mark's rooms.

But even if she seemed to have given a fair quantity of her time to family, Margaret Thatcher also worried about the *quality* of it. She reportedly worried about her mental engagement with her loved ones. In her later years, she reportedly feared being elsewhere mentally and thinking on other things, even in the presence of family.

The twins Carol and Mark are not close to each other. Blood relations did not automatically mean closeness after all. As

Carol once said, "*You need to have something in common.*"

Whether or not this had anything to do with how they were raised is unknown. As for their relationship with their mother… In Margaret Thatcher's years of decline, the twins were not a frequent presence in her life. Carol had once said something along the lines of it being too much to expect grown-up children "*to boomerang back*" enough to allow an absentee mother to "*make up for lost time.*"

Margaret Thatcher, who could be very pragmatic, probably understood what her life in politics cost her in the end. In a magazine interview in her later years, she was quoted as saying – "*you can't have everything.*"

She described holding the position of Prime Minister of the country as "*the greatest privilege,*" while recognizing the toll on her family. But in the final balance, she still seemed comfortable about her life choices, saying – *"I can't regret."*

Legacy

Margaret Thatcher had paid the price for her political service and inextricably, political ambition. She made her mark and then was forced down, even as she had already made sacrifices in her personal life. But she still had a lot of life to live after being Prime Minister.

Life after 10 Downing Street

Political image recovery came for Margaret Thatcher when the ERM collapsed and her Conservative successor John Major proved competent in economic management of the country. When some of her concerns proved right after all, she regained standing within her own party too.

Internationally, her star shone brightly as well. She became an in-demand (and extremely well-compensated) speaker at home and abroad.

She also worked heavily on humanitarian concerns. She was outspoken about the genocide in the former Yugoslavia. She did fundraising for The Margaret Thatcher Foundation's variety of causes.

In 1992, Margaret Thatcher made her way into the House of Lords as Baroness Thatcher of Kesteven. Somehow she found time to author several books about her life, her work, and her craft.

Just as the title suggests, *The Downing Street Years* (1993) chronicled her time holding the office of the Prime Minister. *The Path to Power* (1995) was an account of her early life. *Statecraft* (2002) was about international affairs.

She was getting on in years by her third tome, however, and suffered several mini-strokes. She had to back away from speaking engagements due to frail health.

She also suffered a number of heartbreaks around the same time. 2003 saw the death of her beloved Denis, her "*golden thread*" with whom she had been married for over fifty years, since 1951. Shortly afterwards also saw the death of her close friend and ally, former U.S. President Ronald Reagan.

2005 at least saw a celebration, for her 80th birthday. A celebration held in her honor was even attended by Tony Blair and Queen Elizabeth II herself.

Her deteriorating health started regularly hitting the news by the 2010s. She missed her 85th birthday celebration, hosted by David Cameron, at Number 10. She missed the 2011 wedding of Prince William, the same year that her office located at the House of Lords was shuttered for good. She retreated from the public eye, and lived quietly in London with a failing memory.

Baroness Margaret Thatcher passed away in April 2013 at the age of 87. Her death by stroke marked the end of years of struggle with illness.

A Mixed Legacy

When she died, she held the record as longest serving Prime Minister of the United Kingdom in the 20th Century… she was also the only female (she wouldn't be followed by another until many years after her death, by Theresa May in 2016).

When she died, she was greatly mourned. Not just a leader, as had been said by then Prime Minister David Cameron – a savior. She stood up stalwartly against communism. Her "Iron Lady" nickname, it must be remembered, had come from Soviet journalists… and she reportedly liked it. In this and in other ways she was a strong leader. She was certainly perceived as such by her own countrymen too.

After all, she also came into position with willpower and a coherent vision, at a time when her country had firmly declined from empire to *"the sick man of Europe."*

There were strikes and protests aplenty – ambulance services, nurses, electricians and so on – that left a lot of public services paralyzed. Schools had to be shuttered. BBC and ITV were taken off the air for a time. Trash was piling in the streets. The Government was contemplating a State of Emergency.

"There's no future in England's dreaming," sang the Sex Pistols at the time – it was not an isolated perspective. *"Britain is a tragedy,"* opined iconic U.S. statesman, Henry

Kissinger. As for the ordinary Briton on the street? Many emigrated away.

Margaret Thatcher came in with big plans and a strong political will, and helped bring about changes, many of them irreversible. A lot of them worked towards improving the lot of many of her countrymen, even if the remedy did sting for a time and there were and continues to be avenues for error and abuse.

Perhaps at times she was too stern in dispelling bitter medicine to the economically ailing country she inherited. Some of her policies have been described as heartless. She may have also been too idealistic about individual morals and the transformative power of a free market in bettering society.

At any rate, her loss was mourned but also brazenly celebrated – even hotly anticipated by some corners. Impromptu street parties, chanting and even sharing of cake broke out in some neighborhoods upon news of her death. Many pubs held happy hours, some even hosting Thatcher-era miners who had participated in their infamously drawn-out strike. There was actually a website put up called *Is Thatcher Dead Yet?*, and someone else had established a social media campaign to bring *Ding Dong! The Witch is Dead* (from *The Wizard of Oz*) back into the music charts.

It is unsurprising that she is both so fervently loved and hated.

Margaret Thatcher's politics could be very severe, and she sometimes had a very stark way of looking at things. The miners' strike, for example, she had actually compared to the Falklands War. "*We had to fight the enemy without…We always have to be aware of the enemy within.*" And 'enemies within,' she said at the time, could be harder to fight and be "*more dangerous to liberty.*" She was talking about miners from her own country.

She weakened trade unions. She suppressed the miners' strike. Some of her economic policies hurt communities for generations. Her term saw a dramatic spike in unemployment. Her policies tore into the British manufacturing industry, and some of the neighborhoods that depended on it never quire recovered. Heavy deregulation of the financial sector proved a risky enterprise.

Aside from economic hardware, the changes she helped bring about have also been blamed for softer, harder to quantify, cultural effects.

Did she help spur a more individualistic culture of selfish, opportunistic people with no care for anyone other than themselves? One with little society or community? Did she leave behind a country more divided, where some people had to be thrown under the bus for her brand of economic recovery through the free market?

If she did, was it even worth it? Did the irreversible elements of Thatcherism succeed and if it did, does it still work?

Since the end of World War II, three massive economic collapses have occurred, all of them after Thatcherism. Pundits attribute this to a deregulated financial sector with a decimated industrial base. Britain's industrial heartlands never really picked up again, to the continuing detriment of some communities.

Decreased trade union power, which stemmed from anti-union laws and high unemployment, decreased the bargaining power of workers with many in the working class left poor even when businesses did well. By some observers, the country eventually became more unequal, and this is the unfortunate reality lived by many today.

Margaret Thatcher was also on the wrong side of history on a number of international issues. She likened the South Africa apartheid fighters, the Africa National Congress to terrorists and did not support sanctions on the apartheid state. She also received criticism for entertaining alleged Chilean human rights abuser, General Augusto Pinochet, in London.

Margaret Thatcher also fell short of feminist hopes. She was a female, unabashedly womanly and self-aware of her strengths as one. She was female role model, but not a feminist. Her rise was the personal success of an individual who was almost incidentally a woman; it was not a herald of success or a stepping stone for womanhood. Even in an area where she had immediate sphere of influence – her cabinet – she promoted just one female in over a decade. What she did for women was perhaps almost by incident of her existence as an inspiration rather than by her conscious design.

She left behind a complicated legacy. We cannot definitively say how good she was for women entering into politics. Similarly, we do not know exactly if she really saved her country and if her economic and political philosophy is the right one, the right one at the time, or the right one for us now. But that is perhaps the nature of governance. It is dynamic, it can be dirty, and all too often there are no simple answers, no universal solutions, no easy paths. It is not a precise science and yes, mistakes will be made.

When once asked about regrets, Margaret Thatcher had mused on cutting taxes for the rich. *"I thought we would get a giving society, and we haven't."*

She trusted individuals to act upon the same social duties she expected of herself, and they fell short. Her trust in a person's sense of moral responsibility and of individual decisions tempered by a sense of accountability to society and to God, did not adequately consider love of money and wealth, or greed, or accumulation and conspicuous consumption.

If this was her failure, it must also be considered a shortcoming of individuals who could have contributed so much more to the larger society, and did not. It may have been too idealistic to believe in, but it was also a larger human failure that we couldn't live up to that ideal.

Margaret Thatcher has a mixed legacy that in this day and age is still debated. She is not likely to mind it. She was, after all, once quoted as saying:

"If you just set out to be liked, you would be prepared to compromise on anything at any time, and you would achieve nothing."

She was and is not universally liked, a fact which was probably well-known to her when she was alive. But what even her detractors could not doubt, was that she was a woman of steely conviction, commitment and action.

For all of its good and bad, she was indeed a true "Iron Lady."

Winston Churchill

Blood, Toil, Tears and Sweat: A True Account of the Life and Times of the UK's Greatest Prime Minister

Michael Woodford

Table of Contents

A State Funeral

In the United Kingdom the pomp and ceremony of a state funeral is habitually accorded only to monarchs. Even their consorts are not, strictly speaking, given state funerals.

There are a handful of non-royals, commoners even, who have been given state funerals as a tribute for the service they rendered their country.

Among these notables is Sir Isaac Newton the eminent scientist, Horatio Nelson, who saved England from invasion, the Duke of Wellington, who defeated Napoleon at the Battle of Waterloo, as well as William Ewart Gladstone, one of Britain's greatest prime ministers.

The last state funeral was held on January 30 1965. It was the largest state funeral in the United Kingdom's history and one of the largest the world has ever seen.

Emissaries from 112 countries came to mourn and 350 million people worldwide saw the funeral on television.

The monarch, a youthful Elizabeth II, was very much alive, and, breaking tradition, she attended the funeral herself. Such was the awe in which the nation held the deceased.

This was of course the funeral of Sir Winston Churchill (1874 – 1965), arguably the greatest Prime Minister Britain has ever had. He led the country through its greatest trial.

There are many however who would vigorously contest this assessment. He is accused of being a warmonger; of promoting imperialism and notions of white superiority.

Others see him as an anti-Semite or anti-unionist. Yet others see him as a man of contradictions, both gifted and flawed.

Love him or hate him, it is impossible to ignore his iconic status.

Winston Leonard Spencer-Churchill, to give him his full name, came from a prestigious family whose ancestors figured powerfully in the life of Britain.

John Churchill, the first Duke of Marlborough (1650 – 1722) had been a soldier and a statesman.

His prowess on the battlefield had secured the throne for James II when he suppressed the Monmouth Rebellion in 1685.

However, it is names like Blenheim and Malplaquet that have secured John Churchill a place in the history books. He gave Britain victory after victory in the War of the Spanish Succession (1702 – 1715).

But it was really the friendship of his wife, Sarah Jennings, with Queen Anne (1702 – 1714) which gave him a voice at court.

Under Anne's benevolence the Churchill family became the wealthiest in England.

John had influence in the courts of continental Europe as well.

Lord Randolph Spencer-Churchill, Winston's father, was the third son of the seventh Duke of Marlborough, John Winston Spencer-Churchill (the title passed to the Spencer's through marriage and yes, the families of Winston Churchill and Princess Diana Spencer are related).

Randolph was a statesman of some note. He was a Tory but he believed that the Conservatives ought to lead social reform rather than leave that ground to the Liberals.

Lord Salisbury invited him into his cabinet to serve as Secretary of State for India in 1885. In the following year he became Chancellor of the Exchequer.

The top job, the prime ministership, evaded him however. He resigned over a dispute with the cabinet, soon after his health declined. He died in 1894 from weakness brought on syphilis. He was 45.

Randolph Spencer-Churchill was an intense, passionate man. Although he was charming in company he had no capacity for compromise and no consideration for the feelings of others, especially his political opponents.

Winston's mother was Jennie Jerome (1854 – 1921). She was born in Brooklyn, New York.

Jerome knew Randolph through the Prince and Wales and future King Edward VII and they became engaged only 3 days after their meeting.

Jerome was a vivacious woman. She was close friends with the Prince of Wales, who was well known for his appetite for the company of beautiful women.

The exact relationship of the Jerome and the Prince remains unclear, though it is known that after Randolph's death the Prince addressed her as 'ma chere'. She apparently called him 'Tum Tum.'

The habit of royalty marrying off their favorites to keep them close to court is also well known.

Indeed Jerome was supposed to have taken many lovers during her marriage to Lord Randolph, including Herbert von Bismarck, the son of the celebrated Iron Chancellor of Germany.

It should be noted that Lord Randolph had many enemies, as did his more famous son, and so it would not be hard to imagine Jerome's reputation being exaggerated.

Like most of the aristocracy of the day Lady Spencer-Churchill spent little time with her children.

Nevertheless Winston adored her.

He was also very close to his favorite nanny, Elizabeth Everest (1832-1895).

The daughter of a Cumberland clergyman, Everest entered into service with the Churchills in 1875, a few months after Winston was born.

Winston idolized his mother but as a distant goddess. He received warmth from West and placed all his confidences in her.

On one occasion Winston was to make a speech at Harrow School. Neither of his parents could spare the time to support their son.

Everest could, however. After the speech a proud Winston walked his nanny around the college on his arm.

She was abruptly sacked by the Churchills in 1893 and Winston lost the one source of real love in his childhood.

Perhaps the Churchills were jealous of her influence on their son. Or perhaps they feared it.

After Everest died of peritonitis Churchill spent large amounts of money to keep flowers on her grave.

Winston had one sibling, John. He was born in 1880, four years after Winston.

His mother's sisters believed that John's father was Evelyn Boscawen, son of the 6th Viscount Falmouth.

Given the extraordinary similarity between Winston and John this would seem difficult to credit.

John served with distinction in the Army and died in 1947.

Winston was also intended for the Army. At the time the military was a path to status and influence, and the sons of the aristocracy inevitably became officers.

Winston Churchill tried to join Sandhurst College three times. It was only on the fourth attempt that he finally passed the entrance exam.

He had not excelled in school and so applied for the cavalry rather than the infantry. The educational standard of cavalry officers was not as high as that of the infantry.

In 1894 he graduated and was commissioned as a cornet or second lieutenant in the 4th Queen's Own Hussars.

The Queen's Own was a highly decorated unit and traced its origins to a regiment of dragoons raised to suppress the Monmouth

Rebellion in 1685. They would have fought with Churchill's illustrious ancestor the 1st Duke of Marlborough.

In 1895 Cuban insurgents rose against the Spanish, their colonial overlords.

Churchill obtained permission to go to Cuba and observe the conflict from the Spanish position and write about it for Daily Graphic newspaper. A fellow officer, Reginald Barnes, accompanied him.

He came under for the first time in Cuba and received a Spanish medal for valor.

He enjoyed his experience in Cuba but was transferred to Bangalore, India in 1896.

There Churchill met his first love, the fabulous beauty and socialite Pamela Plowden. He proposed, but he was only 22 and a junior officer.

When Plowden married Victor Lytton, son of the Viceroy of India in 1898 he was heartbroken.

In his grief he threw himself into reading, especially on politics. He read Gibbon, McCauley and Plato and other authors.

He thought about studying historic and politics at university, but he had not achieved the standard of Greek and Latin required for the entrance exam.

The two years in India were formative ones for Churchill. He developed his opinion of religion and in particular the established Church of England, i.e., that it served as a moral crutch for people not ready to rely on reason alone.

His political views were also defined during this period. His mother, desiring his son to abandon the military and enter politics, sent him copies of parliamentary debates, which he would read with interest and then write his own opinion of the matters debated.

On the political spectrum he was, like his father, a Conservative who believed that Tory governments should lead social reform.

This political philosophy, coined 'Tory Democracy' by the eminent Conservative Prime Minister Benjamin Disraeli, takes a paternalist stance toward government. It believes it is the responsibility of the privileged classes to better the lives of the governed.

Not a very radical philosophy, we might say today. However, juxtaposed to the prevailing conservativism of the day, which held that society ought to evolve gradually and organically without any impulse from government, it certainly was a radical notion.

Tory democracy or 'one nation conservatism' as it is also called, is, arguably, the position of the UK Conservative Party today.

In 1897 another war broke out, this time in the region of north-west India we now call Pakistan.

The tribes of the region were self-governing but under British protection. They feared outright annexation and so rose up.

On the June 10 1897 a detachment of Indian troops were escorting a British officer through the Tochi Valley near the frontier.

They were set upon by a tribe called the Mohmands.

Attacks on British forts soon followed.

During the campaign against the tribesmen Churchill served as a scout.

Sighting the enemy, he and fourteen other scouts were fired upon. They waited for the arrival of troops.

When British troops arrived a fierce battle ensued. During the fight a British officer was wounded.

He was dragged away by British soldiers but they had to abandon the officer under heavy fire. An enemy soldier then killed the officer as a horrified and outraged Churchill looked on.

The fighting continued for another two weeks.

During this campaign he found time to write articles for newspapers and to complete his first book, The Story of the Malakand Field Force, a description of the campaign.

In 1898 Churchill went to the Sudan, where the Mahdist War was under way.

Muhammad Ahmed bin And Allah, the self-proclaimed Mahdi ('Guided One') of Islamic prophesy lead a war against the Khedive of Egypt, who ruled the Sudan with his imperial overlords, the British.

Churchill participated in the Battle of Odurman under the famous Sir Herbert Kitchener.

The battle was a slaughter. 12000 Mahdists died and the British lost only 47 men.

While on service there Churchill sent accounts of the war to the Morning Post. After the Sudan Churchill return to England, he resigned from the British Army in 1899, being more interested in war journalism and politics.

In 1899 he ran for a seat in Parliament.

Robert Ascroft was one of the sitting members for Oldham. Oldham was unusual in that returned two members to Parliament.

Ascroft, a Conservative, had previously asked Churchill to stand as a successor for the second MP, James Oswald.

However, Ascroft became seriously ill and was forced to resign his seat. The Party then asked Churchill to run for Ascroft's seat.

Churchill was not elected, losing to the Liberals.

He was not routed however. The two Liberal candidates won the election with 26.7 and

26.2 percent of the vote respectively. Churchill gained a not unimpressive 23.5.

Churchill was not disheartened. He just had to find another way to advance his political career.

In October 1899 the Second Boer War broke out being Great Britain and the Boer Republics of southern Africa.

The Boers were farmers of Dutch descent. They spoke Afrikaans, a Dutch dialect and were highly suspicious of the British, who occupied Cape Colony on the southern tip of Africa. The Cape had been settled by the Dutch in the 17th century.

The British had interests in the Republic of South Africa and the other Boer Republic.

The defense of these interests became greater after the discovery of diamonds in the republics.

The armed Boer farmers proved a match for the British, and Lord Kitchener, the British commander, resorted to draconian measures to secure victory.

He employed a scorched earth policy, burning farms and destroying resources to deny them to the Boers.

Infamously he set up concentration camps, clearing the land of civilians to terrorize the population and deprive Boer soldiers of aid and comfort.

During the war more than 46000 civilians perished. More than 26000 died in the camps.

Public support for the war was not strong in Britain. Discomfort grew when news of Kitchener's atrocities reached home.

On the subject of the British Army's genocidal tactics Churchill was silent. He acknowledged the existence of the camps but wrote that they produced 'the minimum of suffering.'

Meanwhile reports of the appalling conditions in the camps were being read in Parliament and a commission was being set up to investigate the matter.

The truth about Churchill was that he was a lifelong imperialist.

Loyalty to the British Empire and its interests was of course nothing new at the time. It was the prevailing sentiment.

However the many statements of Churchill on the subject of imperialism reveal him to be quite brutal and crude in his assessments of the peoples the Empire fought.

Writing of the tribesmen in North-west India he stated that they had an 'aboriginal propensity to kill.'

During the Sudan conflict he boasted of killing three 'savages.'

Later, as an MP, he advocated further expansion of the Empire, saying 'the Aryan stock is bound to triumph', words familiar in the mind of one infamous future adversary.

In the 1920s when he was Colonial Secretary, he openly advocated gassing Kurdish rebels. 'I am strongly in favor of using poisoned gas against uncivilized tribes,' he said. He felt it would 'spread a lively terror.'

Churchill returned to Britain something of a war hero. He had been captured by the Boers and escaped.

The Boer War ended in 1902. In 1902 Churchill joined the Imperial Yeomanry, a volunteer reserve unit created for service in the Second Boer War. He was commissioned a captain.

He had also made inroads in his political career. In 1900 he stood again for Oldham and was this time returned for the Conservative Party.

His maiden speech in Parliament was made on February 18 1901. It was made entirely without notes and was a powerful display of the rhetorical prowess for which he would be famous.

He used the speech to criticize David Lloyd George, the future Liberal Prime Minister, who had just criticized the conduct of the Boer War.

He said 'The hon. Member [Lloyd George] dwelt at great length upon the question of farm burning. I do not propose to discuss the ethics of farm burning now; but hon.

Members should, I think, cast their eyes back to the fact that no considerations of humanity prevented the German army from throwing its shells into dwelling houses in Paris, and starving the inhabitants of that great city to the extent that they had to live upon rats and like atrocious foods in order to compel the garrison to surrender. I venture to think His Majesty's Government would not have been justified in restricting their commanders in the field from any methods of warfare which are justified by precedents set by European and American generals during the last fifty or sixty years.'

Today we would find such justification of barbarity chilling. It was typical of the mindset that would see Churchill in the highest elected position in the land. It was the mindset that was determined to use any means to see his country victorious in two

world wars.

Laying the Foundation

Churchill did not remain long with the Conservatives. His Tory Democracy ideas clashed with the prevailing Conservative ideology.

He was passionately opposed to protectionism and in 1904 crossed the floor to join the Liberals.

He was not entirely comfortable with the Liberals either, especially on the question of Home Rule for Ireland, which they supported. Nevertheless they seemed to afford Churchill the best hope of furthering his political aims.

In December 1905 Henry Campbell-Bannerman became Prime Minister. He was made Under-Secretary of State for The Colonies under the Secretary, Lord Elgin.

Elgin had been Viceroy of India and held similar views the administration of the col0onies as did Churchill. I Churchill particularly concurred with Elgin over the rejection of a generous peace settlement with the Boers, as Campbell-Bannerman wanted.

In the 1906 general election the Liberals offered Churchill the comfortable seat of Manchester North West, which he won without difficulty.

By now he was one of the most influential members of government outside cabinet. Campbell-Bannerman had wanted to bring

Churchill into the cabinet but the idea had been vetoed by the King, Edward VII.

It was rare for a monarch to use his veto power over the nomination of a minister, even in the beginning of the twentieth century.

As we have seen, the relationship of the Churchill's and the Royal House of Saxe-Coburg and Gotha was at times more intimate than society could tolerate.

Churchill's mother had been Edward's mistress. Furthermore Edward had ordered Lord Randolph Winston's brother, the Marquis of Blandford to marry the Countess of Aylesford, one of the royal mistresses.

It was also rumored that Winston was in fact Edward's son.

It is unclear that any of this played into the decision to refuse Churchill a cabinet post. In any case the King found it impossible to later appoint him President of the Board of Trade, a post that brought him into the Cabinet.

As President of the Board of Trade, Churchill could pursue social reforms. He introduced an 8 hour working day for miners, introduced a minimum wage for the first time in Britain, and introduced labor exchanges to help people find work.

Churchill was prominent in supporting the People's Budget of 1911, which taxed high incomes in order to fund social welfare programs. The Budget was controversial, blocked by the House of Lords and not passed until the Liberal Government won a general election.

In 1911 Churchill pushed for Parliament to pass measures that would place 'mental defectives' in what would effectively be labor camps.

Furthermore, he believed that all inmates of these camps should be sterilized to preserve the integrity of the population.

This idea astounds us, coming from the mouth of someone who was to lead Britain in the fight against someone obsessed by the idea of racial purity.

The idea of protecting the population by such measures was in fact widespread at the time and would remain until the 1950s, if not later.

State-sponsored eugenics was also widespread in western countries, and, with the possibilities offered by modern genetics, the idea seems to be reviving in our day.

The writer and orator G.K. Chesterton was fiercely opposed to Churchill, describing the proposed bill as endorsing slavery and degradation.

He also felt the bill was so vague that any number of people society disliked might be caught by it and institutionalized.

In 1913 the Mental Deficiency Act was passed with only three MPs opposing it.

Churchill was not able to pass the sterilization measures, but the Act was to place 65,000 persons, deemed unfit to live in society, in 'colonies', forever separated from their loved ones.

In 1910 Churchill was appointed Home Secretary, a key cabinet post that gave him management of the internal affairs of the United Kingdom.

His tenure as Home Secretary was controversial. He personally intervened in a number of crises, the most controversial.

In 1910 coal miners rioted in the Rhondda Valley over an industrial dispute. Churchill personally ordered the Army to join the police to quell the disturbance. This lead to much ill-feeling against Churchill in Wales.

Then there was an incident early in January 1911. The siege of Sydney Street, also called the Battle of Stepney, involved a gunfight between police and army on one side, and two Latvian revolutionaries on the other.

Just after shooting began the police were amazed to find the Home Secretary in their midst. They were even more amazed to hear Churchill issuing operational commands, though Churchill would later deny this.

The building where the two men were in caught fire. How it did so has not been determined.

When the senior officer of the Fire Brigade asked permission to extinguish the flame, Churchill refused.

Churchill later wrote 'I told the fire-brigade officer on my authority as Home Secretary that the house was to be allowed to burn down and that he was to stand by in readiness to prevent the conflagration from spreading.'

The two men perished. A subsequent investigation of the incident was critical of Churchill's presence.

Newsreels showing the siege were booed by audiences when Churchill appeared.

Churchill however was confident of himself. 'I thought it better to let the house burn down rather than spend good British lives in rescuing those ferocious rascals,' he said.

Such remarks were reminiscent of those made about the Boers or Indian rebels. In any conflict the foreigner was always the enemy.

As Home Secretary Churchill had to deal with the Suffragette Movement. It has often been supposed that he was against women having the vote.

It is true that he deplored the disturbances occasioned by the protests of the suffragettes. Yet he was in favor of putting the question to a referendum, and his own wife was passionately in favor of votes for women.

Clementine Hozier married Churchill on September 12 1908. Born in 1888, she was the daughter of Sir Henry Montague Hozier and

Lady Blanche Hozier, a daughter of the 10th Earl of Arlie.

Winston and Clementine met at a ball in 1904, though it was not until 1908 that they began courting.

They loved each other deeply, though the marriage was a turbulent one. Churchill could be selfish and impulsive, and Clementine sometimes considered divorce.

Then again, Clementine was no mere doormat. She crossed and contradicted her husband on many occasions, particularly on political issues, though never in public.

Churchill was afraid of her wrath, referring to her privately as 'She-whose-commands-must-be-obeyed.'

Nevertheless she was Churchill's emotional rock and mainstay. Her intelligence and courage complemented that of her husband, though she was a powerhouse in her own right.

'I hope you will not be very angry with me for having answered the suffragettes sternly,' Churchill wrote to his wife. 'I shall never try to crush your convictions [but] I must claim an equal liberty for myself. I have told them I cannot help them while the present tactics are continued.'

Clementine did however agree that violence was not the way to achieve votes for women.

In the end the idea of a referendum was rejected by Prime Minister Asquith's Government. It would not be until 1928that the franchise would be extended to all women in the United Kingdom over the age of 21.

World War I

Toward the end of the nineteenth century European politics was punctuated by a series of diplomatic incidents that threatened to break a peace that had – with some interruptions that involved only a few countries – lasted since the Battle of Waterloo in 1815.

Equilibrium of sorts had been achieved but it was beginning to unravel.

France, which had been previously isolated diplomatically, concluded an alliance with the Russian Empire in the 1890s.

Further, Great Britain and France signed the Entente Cordiale with France. The Entente was not a formal alliance. It did however signify diplomatic cooperation between the two powers.

The object of these two agreements was Germany, and to a lesser extent, its ally the Austro-Hungarian Empire.

France both feared and wanted war with Germany. In 1871 France had been defeated by the superior German Army and had been forced to cede the border province of Alsace-Lorraine.

The mood in France was for revenge and a desire to check the German menace forever.

Russia had been an ally of Germany but it had interests in the Balkan Peninsula. The Balkans was composed of a number of small nations, as it is now, all with conflicting interests. It was a time bomb waiting to explode (again, as it is now).

The moribund Austro-Hungarian Empire, jointly dominated by Germans and Hungarians, was Russia's rival for influence in the Balkans, and Germany was the Empire's staunch ally.

Britain had previously adopted a policy of 'splendid isolation', a sort of armed neutrality yet working behind the scenes to set power against power in defense of British interests.

By the beginning of the twentieth century however Britain felt it could no longer rely on its great fleet, the largest and most powerful in the world, to protect its empire.

This was because Germany, the greatest industrial power on the continent, was building a fleet to rival that of Britain.

War erupted in the Balkans in 1912 and again the following year. The great powers however had managed to contain it.

So when in 1914 a fresh crisis occurred in the Balkans the British public generally assumed that the diplomats would stave off war once again.

On June 28 1914 the heir to throne of Austria-Hungary, Archduke Franz Ferdinand of Austria was shot dead with his wife Sophie in the town of Sarajevo, Bosnia-Herzegovina, then under Austro-Hungarian rule.

His assailant was a Serbian nationalist by the name of Gavrilo Princep.

After the assassination there was a flurry of diplomatic activity between the Great Powers of Europe.

Austria-Hungary gave Serbia, blamed for the assassination, an ultimatum it could not possibly have accepted. Austria-Hungary declared war on Serbia.

Serbia was a small country with no capacity to resist a full scale attack. Russia came to Serbia's aid and declared war on Austria-Hungary.

Germany, supporting its only powerful ally, declared war on Germany.

By August 3, when Germany declared war on France, pre-empting a French attack in support of Russia, a full-scale European conflict was under way.

Britain however, was still uncommitted, despite the Entente Cordiale.

The British Foreign Secretary, Sir Edward Grey, had attempted to mediate between the powers but to no avail. Britain had no direct interest in the Serbian affair, though Grey declared that 'if, however, war does take place, the development of other issues may draw us into it, and I am therefore anxious to prevent it.'

At the time Churchill was First Lord of the Admiralty. He had been appointed to the post in October 1911.

The First Lord was the political head of the Royal Navy with responsibility for its management. The post no longer exists.

The position was a powerful and onerous one. The British Empire depended upon the superiority of its navy. Whoever controlled the Navy controlled the Empire.

The First Lord of the Admiralty was only responsible to the Sovereign and Parliament.

At first Churchill supported Grey's efforts to prevent war. He was in favor of British neutrality.

The British cabinet did however promise to use the Navy to protect France's coastline from attack and the French Government took this a full commitment to France.

On August 4 Germany declared war on the little nation of Belgium, after it refused to allow troops to pass through its territory to invade France.

The British Cabinet was expecting this, yet hoping against hope that it would not occur. In the face of such a flagrant violation of international law it would be hard not to intervene.

Another factor to consider was Belgium's proximity to Britain. Belgian ports might become bases for German warships and form the basis of a trade blockade against Britain.

Britain gave Germany an ultimatum: withdraw from Belgium or Britain would declare war.

Churchill described the scene at the Admiralty when the ultimatum expired on August 4 1914.

'It was eleven o'clock at night – twelve by German time – when the ultimatum expired. The windows of the Admiralty were thrown wide open in the warm night air. Under the roof from which Nelson had received his orders were gathered a small group of admirals and captains and a cluster of clerks, pencils in hand, waiting. Along the Mall from the direction of the Palace the sound of an immense concourse singing 'God save the King' flouted in. On this deep wave there broke the chimes of Big Ben; and, as the first stroke of the hour boomed out, a rustle of movement swept across the room. The war telegram, which meant "Commence hostilities against Germany", was flashed to the ships and establishments under the White Ensign; all over the world. I walked across the Horse Guards Parade to the Cabinet room and reported to the Prime Minister and the Ministers who were assembled there that the deed was done.'

Churchill was in his element. He thrived on conflict.

In October 1914 he sent a brigade of Royal Marines to aid in the defence of the Belgian city of Antwerp. When Antwerp fell the barely-trained brigade was captured. Churchill received much criticism at the time for this action.

His greatest blunder of the war (for which he cannot take all of the blame) was undoubtedly the Dardanelles Campaign of 1915.

The Dardanelles is the narrow strait that separates Europe from the Middle East. Both sides of the strait were controlled, as they are now, by Turkey, then known as the Ottoman Empire.

The Ottoman Empire was an ally of Germany.

In November 1914 Churchill conceived a plan to attack the Dardanelles with warships and a small number of troops.

It was hoped that this operation would divert Turkish troops which were fighting the Russians in the Caucasus Mountains. It was also believed that the neutral Balkan countries of Greece and Bulgaria would be emboldened to attack the Ottomans.

Further, securing the Dardanelles would allow Britain and France to send supplies to the ill-prepared and equipped Russian Army fighting the Germans and Austro-Hungarians.

It was planned that troops landing in the Gallipoli Peninsula, on the European side of the strait, would knock out the defenders and then takes the capital of the Ottoman Empire, Constantinople (now called Istanbul), and some 315 km away.

The plan, put into effect from February 1915, failed spectacularly.

Churchill did not expect any serious resistance at sea, using obsolete warships for the operation, and they failed to enter the Dardanelles, which were too well-defended.

After the failure of the fleet however the Admiralty continued with the rest of the plan, landing almost half a million British, French and colonial troops on the Gallipoli Peninsula on April 25 1915.

Again, Churchill had underestimated the strength and capability of the Turkish defense. The troops failed to break through Turkish lines. However it was not until January that the order was finally given to withdraw the troops.

About 194 000 men died. More than 3000 died of disease.

From the beginning the campaign had been hampered by poor planning, the lack of clear objectives, the inexperience of the troops (Churchill had not believed he needed seasoned soldiers), lack of intelligence and lack of adequate equipment.

At home the Government was eager to shift direct blame for the tragic blunder away from it. Prime Minister Herbert Asquith convened the Dardanelles Commission to investigate the causes of the disaster.

The final report, published in 1919, a year after the war ended, laid most of the blame on Churchill.

Even before then, however. Indeed, during the very campaign itself criticism of Churchill mounted.

The First Sea Lord, who directly commanded the Navy, Sir John Fisher, resigned over disputes about the conduct of the campaign in May 1915.

Churchill was seen as a political liability, and he was forced to resign when Asquith formed a coalition with the Conservatives at the end of May 1915. The Conservatives would not have Churchill in the Cabinet.

Churchill refused to accept responsibility for the Dardanelles disaster, and indeed. The entire Cabinet had backed the plan.

But the defeat precipitated a political disaster and Asquith needed a scapegoat.

'I am the victim of a political intrigue,' Churchill complained. 'I am finished!'

The Dardanelles might have destroyed Churchill forever. It certainly dogged him right until the Second World War. His political opponents and critics would often taunt him with its memory.

Yet he never attempted to distance himself from the campaign. 'The Dardanelles might have saved millions of lives,' he said. 'Don't imagine I am running away from the Dardanelles. I glory in it.'

After his resignation (He was still a Member of Parliament) Churchill once again took up a rifle and went to France.

H served there as a lieutenant-colonel in the Royal Fusiliers, where he displayed great personal courage.

Churchill's return to the Army was not a flight. It was certainly not a change in career. Rather he saw service in the military as an opportunity to rehabilitate his reputation. He planned to return to British politics in triumph.

In the summer of 1916 Churchill returned to Britain to sit in Parliament. The war was still raging and Asquith was still Prime Minister, though not for long.

In December 1916 the government was again in crisis. Asquith was unable to bring harmony to Liberal-Conservative coalition. War-time stability was vital.

He resigned the prime ministership. He was replaced by David Lloyd George. He faced a formidable task. The Liberal Party had been split between himself and Asquith. The Opposition was now not only the Conservatives who had not been admitted to the Asquith Government, but half the Liberal Party.

Churchill did not lament the end of Asquith. Perhaps smarting from his forced resignation the previous year, he unjustly described him as weak and ineffectual.

Lloyd George brought Churchill into cabinet, mainly to keep him from challenging for the leadership. He was made Minister of Munitions in 1917, a position created during the war in response to a shortage of artillery shells.

In November 11 the terrible war came to an end. Churchill was highly critical of the peace settlement, which placed the entire responsibility for the war on Germany.

In the Treaty of Versailles, signed in 1919, Germany lost all its overseas territories as well as large tracts of Germany itself. Its eastern territories were assigned to the newly created state of Poland. It also lost territory to France and Belgium.

Further it had to agree to downsize its army and fleet so that it would never again pose a threat to any of its neighbors.

Most humiliating of all however was the war guilt clause of the treaty. Germany acknowledged that it had started the war, and therefore, was bound to pay reparations to its enemies.

The British Government had not wanted to be so severe but the French insisted.

Churchill, unashamedly bold as usual, called the Treaty of Versailles 'monstrous' and 'malignant', and in the light of events that were to come, justly so.

In a speech on the Treaty he said 'After four years of hideous mechanical slaughter, illuminated by infinite sacrifice, but not remarkably relieved by strategy or generalship, the victorious allies assembled at Versailles. High hopes and spacious opportunities awaited them. War, stripped of every pretension of glamour or romance had been brought home to the masses of the peoples and brought home in forms never before experienced except by the defeated. To stop another war was the supreme object and duty of the statesmen who met as friends and allies around the Peace Table. They made great errors. The doctrine of self-determination was not the remedy for Europe, which needed then above all things, unity and larger groupings. The idea that the vanquished could pay the expenses of the victors was a destructive and crazy delusion. The failure to strangle Bolshevism at its birth and to bring Russia, then prostrate, by one means or another, into the general democratic system lies heavy upon us today.'

Prime Minister Lloyd George was reluctantly forced to agree. 'I cannot conceive any greater cause of war than that the German people,' he said, 'who have certainly proved themselves one of the most vigorous and powerful races in the world, should be surrounded by a number of small States, many of them consisting of people who have never previously set up a stable system of government for themselves, but each of them containing large masses of Germans clamoring for reunion with their native land. The proposal of the Polish commission that we should place 2,100,000 Germans under the control of a people which is of a different religion and which has never proved its capacity for stable self-government throughout its history must, in my judgment, lead to a new war in the East of Europe.'

His remarks were stunningly prophetic.

Rise to Power

After the war Churchill was made Secretary of State for War and Secretary of State for Air.

As War Minister he was preoccupied with the notion of destroying Communism.

In 1917 the tottering regime of Tsar Nicholas II of Russia was overthrown. The revolution was subsequently hijacked by the followers of Vladimir Lenin. These 'Bolsheviks' set about creating a Communist state.

The Great Powers at war with Germany: Britain, France and the United States, organized, supplied and coordinated the resistance to the Bolsheviks.

The Russian Civil War lasted from 1917 to 1921. Besides Russians it involved anti-Bolshevik forces supplied by Britain, France, the United States, Russia and other countries.

In the course of the conflict the Bolsheviks savagely murdered the Tsar and his family, which horrified the world and especially his cousin, King George V of Great Britain. George had had the opportunity of giving the Russian royal family asylum in England, but rejected it out of fear that the move might provoke revolution at home.

Churchill hated Communism with a passion. He said it was the 'philosophy of failure' and 'the gospel of envy.'

'From the days of Spartacus, Weishophf, Karl Marx, Trotski, Belacoon, Rosa Luxenburg, and Ema Goldman,' he said, 'this world conspiracy has been steadily growing. This conspiracy played a definite recognizable role in the tragedy of the French revolution. It has been the mainspring of every subversive movement during the 19th Century. And now at last this band of extraordinary personalities from the underworld of the great cities of Europe and America has gripped the Russian people by the hair of their head and has become the undisputed masters of that enormous empire.'

He even said that if he had to make a choice between Communism and Nazism he would choose Nazi ideology.

So vehement was Churchill's hatred for Communism that he would devise a plan, code-named Operation Unthinkable, to push on against the Soviet Union after the defeat of Hitler in 1945.

The plan was of course never implemented, but Churchill remained implacable against the perceived threat of Communism.

Churchill was instrumental in securing cabinet support for the intervention in the Russian Civil War, despite indifference in the general population.

At the same he fought against Communism abroad he fought against the Irish closer to home.

He was opposed to Irish independence, as a great many of his political colleagues did. When Ireland declared independence he denounced the act and fiercely supported the war against the Sinn Fein government and the actions of the notorious Black and Tans.

Churchill was however, a keen support of Home Rule for Ireland as his father had been. In 1921 he became Secretary of State for the Colonies and in capacity signed a treaty in 1921 that acknowledged Ireland as self-governing dominion within the British Empire.

Despite Churchill's deep misgivings about the Treaty of Versailles he did not advocate rapprochement with Germany, but rather insisted on closer ties with France.

In September 1923 the Conservatives left the coalition with the Liberals over a crisis in Turkey.

The Ottoman Empire had been carved up between the Great Powers and Greece in a blatant grab for land and wealth. Britain was always protective of its influence in the Middle East and here was a chance to dominate the region.

Once again, the crisis was in the Dardanelles. Turkish troops, intent on creating a Turkish national state out of the ruins of the Empire, marched against British and French troops positioned in the Dardanelles.

The leader of the Turkish nationalist forces, Mustafa Kemal Ataturk, issued an ultimatum. 'Our demands remain the same after our recent victory as they were before,' he said. 'We ask for Asia Minor, Thrace up to the river Maritsa and Constantinople... We must have our capital and I should in that case be obliged to march on Constantinople with my army, which will be an affair of only a few days. I must prefer to obtain possession by negotiation, though naturally I cannot wait indefinitely.'

Lloyd George and the cabinet, among who was of course Churchill, demanded that Turkish troops withdraw and threatened war.

Churchill may very well have been stung by the word 'Dardanelles' and reflexively determined not to be undone again.

However the British commander in the field refused to present the ultimatum.

The British public did not want another war, certainly not after the unimaginable horror of World War I.

The British military did not want war either.

The British removed from Turkey and war was averted. The Government was the only casualty.

When the Liberal's coalition partners withdrew their support from the government Lloyd George was humiliated and a general election ensued.

Churchill stood for the seat of Dundee but failed. During the campaign he fell ill with appendicitis. Besides that, his own Liberal Party was deeply divided.

The Conservatives won the election, with Bonar Law as prime minister in 1922, followed by Stanley Baldwin in 1923.

In 1924 Ramsay MacDonald and the Labor Party obtained government. It was the first Labor government in the United Kingdom's history.

In the same year Churchill was elected the MP for Eppingy.

During the campaign Churchill called himself a 'Constitutionalist.' This term did not denote a new party but rather a commitment to the traditional electoral system of Britain.

Many were wary of Labor and believed that their socialist policies would subvert the constitution of the United Kingdom.

Churchill was of course passionately anti-socialist. This might have been a motivating factor for him returning to party politics.

He did not however go back to the Liberals, which was on the decline and offered little prospect of gaining government.

Instead he joined the Conservatives.

Churchill himself was among the first to accuse him of political treachery and opportunism. 'Anyone can rat,' he says 'but it takes a certain ingenuity to re-rat.' He was referring to his previous defection from the Conservatives to the Liberals.

When Stanley Baldwin succeeded Ramsay in November 1924 Churchill was appointed Chancellor of the Exchequer.

The Chancellor of the Exchequer was the most powerful figure next to the Prime Minister. He managed the nation's economy and determines the United Kingdom's monetary policy.

As Chancellor Churchill made what he admitted to be 'the greatest mistake of my life.'

In 1924 he decided to restore the Gold Standard, by which the national economy became based on a certain fixed quantity of gold.

The Gold Standard had been abandoned by most countries during the war. Churchill, however, that a pre-war economy would restore pre-war prosperity.

Instead there was chronic deflation and widespread unemployment. Industry found that their costs sky-rocketed. There were widespread riots and to the General Strike of 1926.

The General Strike which lasted from May 3 – May 12 involved almost two million workers, outraged by reduction in wages.

Churchill's actions were not the sole cause of the industrial action. After World War I the production of coal ebbed and the price of coal fell.

Churchill's attitude to the strike was characteristically bellicose. He talked of achieving victory over the workers as if they were unruly Boers and organized troops to guard convoys of good from the ports.

Churchill's antagonistic words and actions, exaggerated as they have been, swiftly inflamed the situation, shocking both the public and his own government colleagues.

The General Strike and other issues rapidly estranged him from the rest of the Conservative establishment. He was becoming a liability.

In 1929 the Conservative Government fell, and Ramsay MacDonald was once again invited by King George V to form a government.

This government was a coalition of Labor, the Conservatives, the Liberals and the National Liberal Party.

Churchill, who was seen as too belligerent, immoderate and unwilling to compromise, was not asked to join the government.

Two disastrous decisions – the Dardanelles Campaign and the Gold Standard – had all but destroyed his career.

Churchill had come back to government in 1917. He was confident he would return now. He may have been bellicose and inflexible, but he was also persistent.

He spent the years of political idleness – the 'wilderness years' – writing a biography of his illustrious ancestor and victor at

Blenheim John Churchill and the voluminous History of the English-speaking Peoples.

During this time he also contributed to political debate. It seems strange to us to learn that the great champion of British democracy discussed abandoning universal suffrage in favor of a franchise based on property ownership.

He also weighed in on the debate concerning Indian independence. He was even opposed to India being granted self-government, which was the Government's policy.

He was disgusted by Gandhi, remarking 'It is alarming and also nauseating to see Mr. Gandhi, a seditious Middle Temple lawyer, now posing as a fakir of a type well known in the East, striding half-naked up the steps of the Vice-regal palace ... to parley on equal terms with the representative of the King-Emperor.'

Churchill's attitude toward India severely damaged his relationship with the Conservatives. During the war the government had promise to share power with elected Indian representatives, but Churchill was against any concession to the idea of self-rule.

The Conservative Prime Minister Stanley Baldwin refused to have him in the cabinet in 1935 precisely over this issue.

Churchill continued to lecture the government ab out foreign affairs. He advocated reconciliation between France and Germany.

Yet this did not stop him warning of German rearmament. As World War II loomed his attitude toward Germany became more and more alarmist. He was fiercely opposed to the policy of appeasement of Prime Minister Neville Chamberlain.

As ever his fear was that Communism would over-run European civilization. When the Japanese invaded Manchuria, a province of China, in 1931, with horrible violence, Churchill preached against the tide of international opinion.

Japan was needed as a bulwark against Soviet Russia, he argued, and China was too weak to resist Russia. So better a strong Japan rather than a weak China on Russia's border.

His attitude toward Fascism was ambivalent. He called Mussolini 'the greatest lawgiver…of all time.' Again, the deciding factor in favor of Mussolini was his anti-Communist stance.

Even Churchill's views about Nazi Germany and its leader were ambivalent.

He disapproved of the nazification of Germany and the treatment of the Jews. Nevertheless of Adolf Hitler he wrote 'One may dislike Hitler's system and yet admire his patriotic achievement. If our country were defeated I hope we should find a champion as indomitable to restore our courage and lead us back to our place among the nations.'

Churchill and Hitler agreed on a number of points.

On the supposed danger presented by the Jews Churchill said 'This movement among Jews is not new ... but a world-wide conspiracy for the overthrow of civilization and for the reconstitution of society on the basis of arrested development, of envious malevolence, and impossible equality.'

Moreover he believed Communism was a creation of the Jewish conspiracy.

Churchill, like Hitler, was a racial supremacist. He declared in 1937 'I do not admit for instance, that a great wrong has been done to the Red Indians of America or the black people of Australia. I do not admit that a wrong has been done to these people by the fact that a stronger race, a higher-grade race, a more worldly wise race to put it that way, has come in and taken their place.'

It must be said that Churchill was certainly not alone in these beliefs. And the difference between him and Hitler was that Churchill balked at following his philosophy to its logical but horrific conclusion. Hitler, however, was not afraid to commit the ultimate evil.

In 1936 the nation and the Empire was rocked by the Abdication Crisis. Edward VIII succeeded his father George V with little enthusiasm or aptitude for the Crown.

When he announced his intention to marry his mistress, the American divorcee Wallis Simpson, Stanley Baldwin told the king that he would not serve if he did so.

Likewise the Liberal leader Archibald Sinclair declared that he would not accept the marriage.

The issue deeply divided the nation.

Churchill was one of the few politicians who publicly supported the king. When Edward considered abdication in order to be able to marry Simpson Churchill urged him to delay.

It would be easy to suppose that Churchill saw the crisis as a means of returning to government. If Baldwin resigned and the opposition refused to form a government, Edward might very well have asked Churchill to do so.

This is certainly what Members of Parliament, who shouted down his speech in support of the king, thought. And indeed, this may have been what Churchill had in mind.

More generous commentators state that Churchill believed the monarchy was essential to a strong Britain, and that an abdication would severely damage the country. He did not favor marriage with Simpson at all, and when Edward VIII did abdicate on December 11 1936 he was swift to back the new king, Edward's brother, George VI.

Nevertheless Churchill had, once again, backed the wrong horse. His reputation had been badly damaged. He faced the possibility of political death.

World War II

In 1939 Neville Chamberlain's patience with Hitler finally gave out. When the Nazi Leader invaded Poland on September 1Britain and France, standing by their guarantee to defend Poland, declared war on Germany.

The war saved Churchill's career. Chamberlain needed a strong, united and able government to face the challenges of war. He felt he had to bring Churchill into government.

He returned to his old job as First Lord of the Admiralty.

He immediately threw himself into action, planning to mine Norwegian waters and then provoke a German invasion of Norway, thus drawing the Germans into a trap whereby that would be defeated at sea.

It had the whiff of the Dardanelles about it and the cabinet refused to agree.

When the invasion of Norway did come the British were not adequately prepared and British forces were forced to withdraw from Norway.

The failure of the Norwegian campaign contributed greatly to Chamberlain's fall. He had been reluctant to actively commit British forces to the conflict, perhaps hoping that even now a peace was possible.

He recognized that he no longer had the support of the public or of his cabinet.

Chamberlain's choice of successor was the Foreign Secretary Lord Halifax. King George VI wanted Halifax. So did the House of Lords, the Labor Part and the Liberal Party.

Churchill in comparison was politically weak. He was a divisive figure. Past actions had brought the government down twice and his tenure as Chancellor of the Exchequer had been disastrous.

Halifax sat in the House of Lords. It had been 37 years since a prime minister had governed from the Lords.

The problem was that while Halifax would be in the House of Lords Churchill would be in the Commons saying whatever he liked. Halifax believed that Churchill would be the de facto prime minister anyway, and so declined the premiership.

With some reluctance Chamberlain and Halifax recommended Churchill to the king.

He was appointed on May 10 1940.

Churchill began his premiership without the backing of the Conservatives or the Establishment, which could not accept the fall of Chamberlain.

There was division in the cabinet. Some including Halifax and Chamberlain (still Leader of the Conservatives), favored negotiations with Germany, particularly after the fall of France in May 1940.

Churchill himself seems to have been dubious about Britain's chances of withstanding an invasion but concluded that the cost of peace would be too high.

In public however Churchill was famously defiant. His famous 'Finest Hour' speech was given in the House of Commons on June 18 1940.

He electrified the Parliament and the people of Britain, galvanizing resistance to the seemingly imminent German invasion and uplifting the spirits of the British people.

His now famous words thundered across the House of Commons 'we shall fight in France, we shall fight on the seas and oceans, we shall fight with growing confidence and growing strength in the air, we shall defend our island, whatever the cost may be, we shall fight on the beaches, we shall fight on the landing grounds, we shall fight in the fields and in the streets, we shall fight in the hills; we shall never surrender.'

Churchill's rhetoric was powerful. It did as much as force of arms to achieve victory. His speeches were defiant and human. In the early days when Britain had few weapons against German military might they gave inspiration to a frightened nation.

He was a popular prime minister. He made many morale-boosting tours, visiting areas devastated by bombs. He remained in London during the Blitz and bolstered the spirit of the nation during the Battle of Britain.

Churchill worked hard, as much as 18 hours a day.

His drive was the more extraordinary given that he suffered from manic depression, or what we would call today bi-polar disorder.

Certain qualities in Churchill's character indicate this disorder. He was belligerent, uninhibited (he would frequently conduct business naked), grandiose, phrenetics and full of energy

He medicated himself with alcohol. His favorite drink was whisky and soda, often drinking as many as 10 during a meal.

His drinking was no secret and he was often observed in an intoxicated state.

He called the depression his 'black dog.' His illness was kept secret from the public of course. They would have been nervous of being lead through their greatest trial by a man who could not approach train platforms for fear he would throw himself in front of a train.

'I don't like standing near the edge of a platform when an express train is passing through. I like to stand back and, if possible, get a pillar between me and the train. I don't like to stand by the side of a ship and look down into the water. A second's action would end everything. A few drops of desperation.'

Much has been made of Churchill's courage and determination during the war years, and justly so, especially given the illness under which he labored.

He has become an icon of British fortitude and pride and because of this it has been hard, even now, to criticize the war leader.

Yet Churchill remained during World War II to same ruthless leader that could recommend the gassing Kurds who dared to oppose British rule and who could order that a building be allowed to burn with people still in it.

He had declared that he sought 'victory – victory at all costs!' On another occasion he remarked 'I have only one aim in life, the defeat of Hitler, and this makes things very simple for me.

Churchill knew of course that Britain could not win the war without the intervention of the United States.

The US Establishment and public was isolationist. It remembered the horrors of World War I and the disaster of the Treaty of Versailles (never ratified by the US Congress).

Recent studies have revealed that President Franklin D. Roosevelt and Churchill conspired to subvert isolationist sentiment in the United States, intercepting communications, spreading rumors, smear campaigns and even kidnapping.

In August 1941 Churchill and Roosevelt met for talks. They issued the Atlantic Charter, a declaration of war aims and a vision of the world after the war

However the United was not actively at war with Germany or Japan.

Thirty years after the event the papers related to that meeting were released, revealing that Churchill and Roosevelt had agreed to much more than what was revealed at the time.

The New York Times wrote on January 2 1972 'Formerly top secret British Government papers made public today said that President Franklin D. Roosevelt told Prime Minister Winston Churchill in August, 1941, that he was looking for an incident to justify opening hostilities against Nazi Germany.... On August 19 Churchill reported to the War Cabinet in London on other aspects of the Newfoundland [Atlantic Charter] meeting that were not made public. ... "He [Roosevelt] obviously was determined that they should come in. If he were to put the issue of peace and war to Congress, they would debate it for months," the Cabinet minutes added. "The President had said he would wage war but not declare it and that he would become more and more provocative. If the Germans did not like it, they could attack American forces.... Everything was to be done to force an incident.'

Churchill was keen to provide such an incident. In 1941 he wrote to Pound, the First Sea Lord, suggesting that a certain German warship be found by American vessels in order to provoke a gunfight between them.

Not soon after, Pound expressed a hope that German that ships escorting American shipping be attacked by German U-boats.

Was Churchill suggesting that innocent lives be endangered so as to provide an excuse for America entering the war?

If so it would not be unprecedented. As First Lord of the Admiralty Churchill had written to the President of the Board of Trade in 1915, stating that it was 'most important to attract neutral shipping to our shores, in the hope especially of embroiling the United States with Germany.'

A week later the Lusitania, a liner carrying American civilians, was sunk by a German U-boat. The sinking contributed to the United States entering the war in 1917.

After an inquiry into the sinking a number of questions were left unanswered.

Why was the Lusitania not escorted by a destroyer, following normal procedure, especially as there were destroyers on hand to do so? Why did the liner reduce speed in a zone known to be patrolled by German U-boats? Did Naval Intelligence know a U-boat was on course to intercept the Lusitania?

These and other questions cannot be definitively answered because many documents relating to the incident are still classified.

However the suspicion is that Churchill and other members of the government and Navy conspired to ensure that the Lusitania was sunk.

Even though there were incidents in the North Atlantic in 1941 these were not enough to provoke the US Congress and public into wanting war.

It was only when Japan attacked Pearl Harbor on December 7 1941 that the United States declared war.

Other incidents during the war demonstrate Churchill's commitment to victory at any coast and his unwillingness to leave anything to chance.

After the fall of France in May 1940 Churchill demanded that France surrender its fleet to the British, lest it fall into German hands.

The French replied that they were going to scuttle the fleet anyway.

This assurance was not good enough for Churchill. Against the advice of the Navy he ordered British ships stationed in the

Mediterranean to open fire on the French vessels.

The French did not resist and 1500 French sailors perished.

Then there were the terror-bombings of German cities.

During these attacks some 600,000 German civilians were killed, with another 800,000 seriously wounded. This is compared with 70,000 civilians killed by German bombers.

The most memorable of the Allied raids is perhaps the bombing of Dresden between February 13 and 13 1945.

It involved 3,900 tons of bombs and created a hellish fire storm that destroyed the city.

The Geneva Conventions forbade the direct targeting of civilian populations during times of war.

On the subject of the target of strategic bombing Churchill declared in the House of Commons that only military equipment and installations were bombed.

This was a lie. The Head of Bomber Command, Arthur Harris, declared that 'the aim of the Combined Bomber Offensive [is] unambiguously stated [as] the destruction of German cities, the killing of German workers, and the disruption of civilized life throughout Germany.'

Churchill admitted as much in the final phases of the war. He sent to a memo to the air commanders 'It seems to me that the moment has come when the question of bombing of German cities simply for the sake of increasing the terror, though under other pretexts, should be reviewed. Otherwise, we shall come into control of an utterly ruined land…. The destruction of Dresden remains a serious query against the conduct of Allied bombing…. I feel the need for more precise concentration upon military objectives … rather than on mere acts of terror and wanton destruction, however impressive.'

After the war Churchill claimed to have no knowledge of the Dresden bombings, instead blaming it on the Americans.

To many these and other deeds were justifiable at the time in order defeat Hitler. To others a war crime is a war crime. Churchill and Roosevelt were purportedly fighting for a world where the rule of law prevailed, as envisaged by the Atlantic Charter, and yet they were prepared to use amoral means to achieve this.

A similar argument occurs today as to how far states are justified in their efforts to protect citizens from Islamist terrorism.

Are means always justified by their ends?

In November 1945 accused Nazis were put on trial for war crimes at Nuremberg.

Churchill had not wanted it. He wanted those declared criminals and then executed without trial.

He gave in to the Americans who regarded open trials as necessary.

Despite Churchill's attitude to what he saw as a Judaeo-Communist conspiracy to subvert civilization he was unambiguous in his condemnation of the Holocaust.

His own war memoirs are oddly silent on the subject, leading many to suppose he tacitly approved of the Jewish persecutions. Yet hi own speeches are quite clear. He categorically deplored the persecution and murder of the Jews.

After the War

The period of the Second World War was glory years for Churchill.

The peace however, was not so kind.

In 1945 there was an election, the first in almost 10 years. The Labor ministers who formed part of the war coalition now refused to support the peacetime government.

Churchill lost the election. The Labor leader clement Attlee became Prime Minister. The people, genuinely grateful to Churchill for the last 6 years perhaps felt they needed a different kind of prime minister in peacetime.

If so, there was some justification for that belief. Churchill was not the kind of leader that would build on national unity. He was belligerent, aggressive and ruthless – qualities better suited to war than peace.

Churchill forgave them. 'They have been through a very hard time,' he said.

Churchill did not retire from politics. The affairs of Britain and the world continued to preoccupy him.

In particular he was concerned that Eastern Europe had fallen under Soviet domination, and was concerned to promote closer ties with the United States to check its advance.

As mentioned in a previous chapter, he had as prime minister wanted allied forces to attack the Soviet Army and drive them from the East.

He also called for a 'United States of Europe' which would be a bulwark against Soviet Russia and a guarantee of European peace.

He had floated the idea as early as 1930. His vision, which would be largely realized in the European Union, would not include Great Britain.

'We are with Europe, but not of it,' Churchill said, a sentiment echoed by the majority of British who voted to leave the European Union.

Churchill remained committed to the British Empire, even though the Atlantic Charter signed with Roosevelt in 1941 promised the right of self-determination to the world's peoples.

But Churchill rejected the universal right of self-determination when it came to the British colonies and in particular to India.

However by the time Churchill was returned to the prime ministership in October 1951 India had already been granted its independence and the Empire was beginning to fragment.

Attlee held government by a slim majority and yielded to the Conservatives.

A new monarch commissioned Churchill to form a government. Queen Elizabeth II had unexpectedly succeeded her father George VI, who had died suddenly.

For Churchill it was business as usual. He seems not to have recognized that the world had changed, and settled on the themes on which he was sure – social reform, war on Communism and the maintenance of the Empire.

In the field of social reform he did much to alleviate the burdens of many people. He raised pensions, reformed housing and increased national assistance schemes.

In colonial affairs he was characteristically belligerent. He declared that he would not preside over a dismemberment of the British Empire. He had no hesitation in employing troops to quell rebellion in Malaya and Kenya.

Churchill had not realized that the United Kingdom had lost its place in the world to the United States. World affairs were now playing out in the context of a struggle between the United States and the Soviet Union.

He felt Great Britain would still play a role as a third superpower in close co-operation with the United States. But Britain's humiliation in the Suez crisis in 1956 (after Churchill retired) demonstrated once and for all that the age of the Empire was over.

How Churchill would have coped with the new age we do not know. He was dogged with ill health. While in office he suffered a stroke.

For a time this was kept from the public. But he could not go on. In 1955 he retired.

Churchill continued in Parliament for a time and continued to comment on national and international affair

It was suggested that he be given title Duke of London, but he declined because his son Randolph had ambitions in politics. Inheriting a dukedom would mean sitting in the House of Lords.

Instead Church was made a Knight of the Order of the Garter.

On the morning on January 24 1965 Churchill suffered a massive stroke and died. He was 90.

Assessment

There is no doubt that Winston Churchill was a giant among men, but how are we to judge his place in history?

He straddled two great ages. He was an Edwardian born into an aristocratic family committed to Empire and the superiority of the British race.

He died in a world which was moving away from colonialism and idea of racial superiority. Indeed it was challenging the very world that Churchill thought he had been defending during the Second World War.

On the one hand it is understandable that he did not see the new world coming, or at least decided that its advance had to be pushed back.

Yet on the other it was a world that he had helped to create by his appeals to freedom and self-determination against fascist tyranny.

But then again he was not completely conservative. He was a social reformer. He believed that governments should lead in reform, a concept that is alien to many conservative politicians and thinkers today.

He was passionate and driven. Yet his passion could lead him to dangerous, even disastrous decisions. He could be driven to ruthless, Machiavellian acts in order to achieve his aims.

This might lead us to wonder what he believed in. Did he believe in Britain and its people, or did he believe in himself?

Churchill was belligerent. He thrived in war. His deeds in peacetime do not stand out and some of his worst decisions were made as a member of the cabinet.

The Churchill we know is a product of war. Some say he was the war leader Britain needed. Others say he was a warmonger.

The lives of the great are often enigmatic. Thousands of books have been written trying to define Churchill. It is doubtful that any one book will. Churchill was a complex figure, not only to us, but possibly to himself as well.

Churchill's Speech to the Nation on the Outbreak of War

Given in the House of Commons September 3 1939

In this solemn hour it is a consolation to recall and to dwell upon our repeated efforts for peace. All have been ill-starred, but all have been faithful and sincere. This is of the highest moral value--and not only moral value, but practical value--at the present time, because the wholehearted concurrence of scores of millions of men and women, whose co-operation is indispensable and whose comradeship and brotherhood are indispensable, is the only foundation upon which the trial and tribulation of modern war can be endured and surmounted. This moral conviction alone affords that ever-fresh resilience which renews the strength and energy of people in long, doubtful and dark days. Outside, the storms of war may blow and the lands may be lashed with the fury of its gales, but in our own hearts this Sunday morning there is peace. Our hands may be active, but our consciences are at rest.

We must not underrate the gravity of the task which lies before us or the temerity of the ordeal, to which we shall not be found unequal. We must expect many disappointments, and many unpleasant surprises, but we may be sure that the task which we have freely accepted is one not beyond the compass and the strength of the British Empire and the French Republic. The Prime Minister said it was a sad day, and that is indeed true, but at the present time there is another note which may be present, and that is a feeling of thankfulness that, if these great trials were to come upon our Island, there is a generation of Britons here now ready to prove itself not unworthy of the days of yore and not unworthy of those great men, the fathers of our land, who laid the foundations of our laws and shaped the greatness of our country.

This is not a question of fighting for Danzig or fighting for Poland. We are fighting to save the whole world from the pestilence of Nazi tyranny and in defense of all that is most sacred to man. This is no war of domination or imperial aggrandizement or material gain; no war to shut any country out of its sunlight and means of progress. It is a war, viewed in its inherent quality, to establish, on impregnable rocks, the rights of the individual, and it is a war to establish and revive the stature of man. Perhaps it might seem a paradox that a war undertaken in the name of liberty and right should require, as a necessary part of its processes, the surrender for the time being of so many of the dearly valued liberties and rights. In these last few days the House of Commons has been voting dozens of Bills which hand over to the executive our most dearly valued traditional liberties. We are sure that these liberties will be in hands which will not abuse them, which will use them for no class or party interests, which will cherish and guard them, and we look forward to the day, surely and confidently we look forward to the day, when our liberties and rights will be restored to us, and when we shall be able to share them with the peoples to whom such blessings are unknown.

Made in the USA
Middletown, DE
17 November 2020